REGIONAL GOVERNMENT IN BRITAIN: AN ECONOMIC SOLUTION?

Alan Harding, Richard Evans, Michael Parkinson and Peter Garside

the POLICY PRESS

First published in Great Britain in 1996 by

The Policy Press
University of Bristol
Rodney Lodge
Grange Road
Bristol BS8 4EA

Telephone: (0117) 973 8797
Fax: (0117) 973 7308
E-mail: tpp@bris.ac.uk

© The Policy Press, 1996

ISBN 1 86134 029 X

All rights reserved: no part of this publication may be reproduced, stored in a retrieval system, or transmitted in any form or by any means, electronic, mechanical, photocopying, recording, or otherwise without the prior written permission of the Publishers.

DURHAM CO ARTS LIBRARIES & MUSEUMS	
5581899	
	17.4.98
352.042	£11.95

Alan Harding is Professor of Urban Policy and Politics at the European Institute for Urban Affairs, Liverpool John Moores University. **Richard Evans** is a Senior Research Fellow at the European Institute for Urban Affairs. **Michael Parkinson** is the Director of the European Institute for Urban Affairs. **Peter Garside** is a Lecturer in Geography at Thames University.

The Policy Press works to counter discrimination on grounds of gender, race, disability, age and sexuality.

Printed in Great Britain by Bourne Press Limited.

Contents

List of abbreviations		v
Acknowledgements		vi
1	**Regions, regionalism and regionalisation: the current debate**	1
	The rise of the region?	1
	Key issues and definitions	3
	The research and the structure of the report	8
2	**The regionalisation of policy making**	10
	Regionalisation described	10
	The rationale for increased regional administration	11
	Boundary definition and coherence	16
	Degrees of regional autonomy	17
	Conclusion	20
3	**Regional economies and regional institutions**	22
	The case studies	22
	Four 'regional economies'	23
	Institutional frameworks in the four regions	39

4	**Institutions, strategies and regional economic competitiveness**	48
	Strategic responses to regional economic problems	48
	Regional institutional capacity: gaps and limitations	57
5	**Regionalisation: the two key questions revisited**	65
	Regionalisation and regional government	65
	Regional institutions and economic competitiveness	66
	Institutions, networks and regional development	74

References	77
Appendix A: Changes in regional activity, 1985-89	83
Appendix B: List of individuals whose views were drawn upon for the study	96

List of abbreviations

CBI	Confederation of British Industry
CoSLA	Council of Scottish Local Authorities
DBRW	Development Board for Rural Wales
GOR	Government Offices for the Regions
GONE	Government Office for the North East
HESIN	Higher Education Support for Industry
HIE	Highlands and Islands Enterprise
LAW	Land Authority for Wales
LECs	Local Enterprise Companies
LiS	Locate in Scotland
NDC	Northern Development Company
NEA	North of England Assembly
NECC	North East Chamber of Commerce
NWBLT	North West Business Leadership Team
NWRA	North West Regional Association
NWRP	North West Regional Partnership
SDA	Scottish Development Agency
SE	Scottish Enterprise
SO	Scottish Office
SOEID	Scottish Office Employment and Industry Department
STI	Scottish Trade International
STUC	Scottish Trades Union Council
WDA	Welsh Development Agency
WO	Welsh Office
WTB	Welsh Tourist Board

Acknowledgements

The research team is indebted to a great many individuals for their help in conducting this study. A number of people were kind enough to burden their very busy schedules still further and serve on the Steering Group for the project. They are:

Michael Appleton, Development Director, English Partnerships

Professor Philip Cooke, Centre for Advanced Studies in Social Sciences, University of Cardiff

David Henshaw, Chief Executive, Knowsley Borough Council

Alastair MacKenzie, Chief Planner, Scottish Office

Geoffrey Piper, Chief Executive, North West Business Leadership Team

John Stoker, Regional Director, Government Office for Merseyside

Terry Thomas, Managing Director, Co-operative Bank

Gavin Watson, Director, Cities, Countryside and Private Finance, Department of the Environment

Steering Group members' advice was particularly valuable at the midway point of the project, when the research team was refining its arguments and developing its case study approach, and again at the end of the study when it came to refining the draft report. Individual members were also very accommodating in helping the research team plan and execute the case study work.

A large number of people from government, local authorities, universities, development agencies, other public bodies, political parties, trades unions, business organisations and individual firms kindly agreed to be interviewed as part of the case study programme. (A full list of these individuals is given in Appendix B.) It was they who provided the 'meat' of the study.

Finally, Pat Kneen, the Principal Research Officer at the Joseph Rowntree Foundation oversaw the development and delivery of the project with efficiency, good humour and understanding.

The usual disclaimer applies. The research team learned a lot from these people. But none of them are responsible for the contents of this report. That burden rests squarely on the shoulders of the authors.

Chapter 1

Regions, regionalism and regionalisation: the current debate

The rise of the region?

Why are regions, regionalism and regionalisation currently attracting so much attention in the UK? Is it largely a question of domestic politics? For example, is the UK system of government simply experiencing one of its periodic challenges from political nationalism within the UK's 'stateless nations' and the enhanced sense of expectation this inevitably creates in the more self-conscious English regions? Or are there signs of a more general unease – a UK-wide popular backlash against the agenda followed by Conservative governments over the past seventeen years? Is regionalisation the political mantra for the 1990s, a more pluralistic successor to its 1980s cousins, centralisation and privatisation? Alternatively, are the key issues more technical than political? Does regional administration make governance easier? Have even those governments who believe fundamentally in the efficacy of their own decisions along with those of the market had to create and extend regional decision-making capacity in recent years to deal with ever more complex problems? Or must we look beyond the UK for explanations? Are there wider and larger forces at play, on the European scale and beyond, which mean that the course of history is somehow running with regions, regionalism and regionalisation and against nations, nationalism and nationalisation? (Harvie, 1994; Cheshire, D'Arcy and Giussani, 1992)

A brief review of recent arguments and reforms suggests that there is evidence within the UK to support each of these propositions. Domestic policy change and administrative restructuring has certainly responded to both territorial and technical demands. The post-1992 Conservative government, for example, has made good on some manifesto commitments developed at the height of the pre-election debate on devolution for Scotland and Wales. A modest programme of regionalisation has been introduced which has seen a small number of Whitehall administrative functions transferred to the Scottish and Welsh Offices (HMSO, 1993; Parry, 1993). New, interdepartmental Government Offices for the Regions (GORs) have also been created in England. And a more explicit regional focus to area-based economic regeneration programmes in England and Wales has been developed as part of the arrangements for the new Single Regeneration Budget (Hogwood, 1995).

At the same time, other government reforms have been interpreted as re-enforcing the arguments for regional government. The continued move towards a single-tier system of unitary local authorities, already in place in Scotland and developing elsewhere, is adjudged by some to create a strategic policy vacuum into which regional government would fit perfectly. Non-Conservative political parties, meanwhile, encourage such debate by remaining committed to regionalisation and/or constitutional change. The Liberal Democrats favour a quasi-federal system of regional assemblies. Labour promises a Scottish Parliament and a Welsh Assembly to oversee the work of the Scottish and Welsh Offices and the option of 'devolution on demand' for the English regions (Labour Party, 1995; Tindale, 1995). Scottish and Welsh nationalist parties, whilst they are drawn to regionalisation as a tactical staging post, look in the longer term towards 'independence in Europe' and the dissolution of the union (SNP, 1992a).

The European angle to the current debate about regions is not just of interest to nationalists. Indeed, quite how UK regions do, could and should take their place within a 'Europe of the Regions' makes the current regional debate in the UK different in tone and substance from its predecessors (Jones and Keating, 1995). The European aspects of the debate operate at different levels. At the more practical end, concern with the power and coherence of regional structures revolves around three issues: a desire to influence EU policy through mechanisms like the Committee of the Regions (CoR); a wish to present a regional voice distinct from national government; and the need to develop regional strategies and coalitions in order to facilitate access to EU regional funding.

The extent to which any of these developments lends support to the case for regional institutional change can be overstated. The Committee of the Regions, for example, plays a relatively insignificant part in EU policy formation. EU regional funds, similarly, are trifling compared to national expenditures within UK regions. And, of course, the influence of regional interests over the European Commission bears no comparison with that wielded by individual nation states, either directly or through intergovernmental mechanisms such as the Council of Ministers (Anderson, 1990). Nonetheless, the need to compete with stronger European regions is keenly felt and has encouraged greater regional networking within, between and beyond UK regions. It has encouraged the move toward Regional Associations of local authorities, the development of regional representation in Brussels and greater participation in transnational network organisations like Eurocities.

At a more conceptual level, a number of arguments suggest that the development of a Europe in which regional decision making plays a larger role may not be too far away. The importance of regional levels of governance may well grow as nation states are forced to change with the times. As economic globalisation deepens and nation states are increasingly unable to perform their traditional, dominant roles in social and economic regulation, a process of 'hollowing out' is occurring (Jessop, 1994). Essentially this means that decision-making power is being reallocated. It is being passed upward, to supra-national institutions, so that problems that no longer respect national boundaries can be managed (Luard, 1990). But it is also passing down to sub-national levels of government (Bennett, 1990). This process inevitably means that the role of the EU becomes more important. At the same time, decentralisation to regions, as in France, Spain and Italy, is seen as going with the grain of the times, whereas centralising tendencies within the UK are seen as out of step, ultimately self-defeating and unsustainable (Crouch and Marquand, 1989).

Regions may also benefit from the economic, as well as the political, implications of globalisation (Harding and Le Galès, 1996). Indigenous economic development and an area's attractiveness to external investors no longer depend so heavily on traditional factors of production. Rather, they rely on new factors more relevant to the information age, including many that are more amenable to public policy influence, such as efficient communication networks, the innovative capacity and advanced labour pools provided by higher education institutions, and quality of life advantages. These public sector inputs need to be attuned to specific production needs and delivered flexibly on an appropriate scale (Mayer, 1994). Since regional 'units' make more economic sense than most European local authority areas, one possible outcome is that the region may come to rival the nation as a sensible unit of supply-side intervention.

Key issues and definitions

It is clear that the current concern with regions, regionalism and regionalisation encompasses a variety of causes and themes. Each of these operates at different levels, has different implications and can lead in different directions. But in the UK debate two core issues outweigh the rest, dominating the concerns of those who have recently resurrected 'the regional question', although they are rarely spelled out or explored systematically. The first is the extent to which governance in the UK has acquired more of a regional dimension in recent years, but without any increase in the democratic oversight of regional decision making. The second is the contested relationship between regional institutional structures and economic dynamism. Both issues are seized upon by proponents of change in the structures of UK government. They form the basis upon which the research for this report was conducted.

It is argued that a regional tier of governance is being created in the UK but that it comprises a non-democratic, fragmented, unaccountable and inefficient 'quangocracy' (Morgan and Roberts, 1993; Davis and Stewart, 1993; Stewart et al, 1995). From this analysis, it is but a short step to the argument that a regional tier of government which would democratise what already exists would simultaneously improve the efficiency and representativeness of governance (Salt, 1994). Other commentators, pointing to an apparent congruence between regional institutional structures and economic dynamism in parts of continental Europe, put forward an economic case for regional government (Murphy and Caborn, 1995). For them, the primary motivation for institutional change is to provide the spur to regional economic competitiveness.

The economic, democratic and technocratic arguments for institutional change are often viewed as mutually reinforcing. It is argued, for example, that a virtuous triangle increasingly links democratic accountability, efficient and effective decision making and economic health at the regional level (European Dialogue/Friedrich Ebert Foundation, 1993). This proposition needs to be subjected to far greater critical scrutiny before it can provide a convincing basis for institutional change. Debate in the UK has not yet produced such a critique. Instead, it remains polarised between those who favour institutional change and those who oppose it.

Proponents of regional government (eg Coulson, 1990) argue that a regional tier of government in England is necessary to enable the decentralisation of functions from the centre already enjoyed to a greater extent in Scotland and Wales. Just as these two stateless nations should be given the opportunity to elect those who run 'their' sub-UK level executive machinery directly, so English regions deserve both the machinery and a similar right of democratic oversight. Only then, they argue, can decision making become better informed and more sensitised to priorities which cannot or will not be recognised by Westminster or Whitehall and its regional outposts. The other major argument is that 'strategic' services should be delivered at a regional scale, thereby eradicating duplication and wasteful competition between local government units which are too small to be effective in some policy areas.

Opponents of regional government (eg Jones, 1988) also base their arguments on the notion of subsidiarity: that functions should be carried out on the most feasible localised scale. But for them that level is the local, not the regional, level. Opponents argue that regional authorities represent an unnecessary tier of elected government between Westminster and what should ultimately be a single tier of unitary local authorities. Scotland and Wales, in their estimation, merit special treatment because they are nations, not regions. By contrast, regional government in England potentially trespasses upon the 'legitimate' functions of national and local governments, makes policy making more complicated by increasing the number of actors in the system, blurs responsibilities and accountability, confuses electorates and limits local government autonomy without achieving anything which could not be achieved more efficiently and effectively by national or local government or through some form of structured, bottom-up, voluntary cooperation.

These sorts of arguments for and against regional government are of long standing. More recent discussions have not added very much to the debate. They have two serious limitations. First, they tend to be vague. Terms like regions, regionalism, regionalisation, regional policy and regional autonomy remain under-defined, and are often used interchangeably with terms such as devolution, deconcentration and decentralisation. Since these terms often mean different things to different people, like is rarely compared with like and the various voices within the debate end up talking past each other. These difficulties are magnified when the focus shifts from the domestic scene to comparison with other nations and their constituent regions.

Secondly, the debate tends to be Anglo-centric and to ignore substantial differences between structures of governance at sub-UK level. The UK is a unitary state in that national sovereignty resides within one Parliament and no sub-national tier of government has constitutional status. However, unlike some other unitary states, it does not have a uniform system of government below national level. In fact, the UK is also a *union* state.[1] Its constituent non-English *nations* have long had special status within the framework of government. It is unwise to compare Scotland and Wales with English regions in terms of their sense of cultural identity, institutional structures, the motivations underlying pressures for institutional and/or constitutional reform and perceptions of which institutional changes are desirable. Northern Ireland is an entirely different case but still, institutionally and culturally, very different from the English regions.

This report and the research that underlies it tried to avoid these pitfalls by defining its terms with some care and by putting the different patterns and structures of governance which already exist at the sub-UK level at the heart of the research programme. When UK *regions* are discussed, the report is referring to the standard regions currently used for official, statistical data collection. With only limited variation, they are the regions first defined for the purposes of national economic planning during the 1960s. This definition is adopted for the sake of simplicity and consistency. But it is necessary to recognise that it combines two types of area. The non-English nations – Scotland, Wales and Northern Ireland – are important units of administration. The standard English regions – the North (including the North East and Cumbria), North West, Yorkshire and Humberside, West Midlands, East Midlands, East Anglia, South East and South West – are not.

Regionalism refers to a state of mind which sometimes becomes an organising principle. It comes in both political/cultural and technocratic forms. Political/cultural regionalists share with others in their region a close cultural affinity which contrasts with, but is not wholly antagonistic to, the dominant national culture. Technocratic regionalists, by contrast, do not concentrate on cultural affinities. Rather, they believe that the cause of good government is best served where regional structures are strong (Garside and Hebbert, 1989). In certain circumstances regionalism results in demands for more regional autonomy. This usually occurs when arguments that regions have consistently been treated unfairly or held back by national government appear to have the greatest validity. Political/cultural regionalism differs in kind from the nationalism characteristic of 'stateless nations'. The latter questions the very legitimacy of the nation state, not just the policies of particular governments (McCrone, 1993). The political expression of nationalism is the desire for independence in the longer term. Regionalism results in claims for a better deal under the existing system.

Regional autonomy is difficult to measure. Essentially, however, it reflects the degree to which major resources – constitutional, legal, financial, human, physical and informational (Rhodes, 1988) – are controlled at regional level. Regional autonomy is best seen in terms of a continuum from high to low rather than as an absolute property which a region either has or does not have. Within government, autonomy is not determined by constitutions or legislation alone (Keating, 1992). It is perfectly possible for a tier of elected government to have constitutional or statutory status but to be relatively weak. The recently-created French regions (Le Galès, 1994) and the Dutch provinces (Toonen, 1993) are examples. Conversely, it is possible that governing arrangements based on administrative devolution can have a relatively high level of autonomy if the other resources vested in them are significant. Some argue this is the case in Scotland (Paterson, 1994). Where constitutional status and independent control over important resources come together, as in the German Länder, then regional autonomy is highest. But it is never absolute.

Whilst the notion of regional autonomy is usually applied to government, decision-making capacity varies according to spatial level in the private sector, too. Executives in corporate branches with a high degree of freedom to commit resources can respond better to regional needs and aspirations than their counterparts in branches whose activities are closely supervised and constrained by distant headquarters. There is controversy, however, about whether it is feasible to talk of regional autonomy in relation to corporate governance (Young et al, 1994; Dicken et al, 1994). The conventional wisdom, symbolised by the notion of a 'branch plant economy', is that regional autonomy in business decision making is simply in terminal decline.

Globalisation intensifies the penetration of local markets by non-local producers and the gearing up of 'local' producers to global market needs. One effect of this is to encourage greater direct inward investment and the buying-out of indigenous firms by 'foreign' corporations, leading to more local economic activity being externally controlled (Turok and Richardson, 1991, on Scotland). Power and control thus pass inexorably from regional actors to corporate headquarters whose commitment to regional economic fortunes is more ambiguous (Amin and Malmberg, 1992). No one disputes the growing influence of transnational corporations over regional economic performance. But other interpretations suggest that symbiotic links between regions and corporations may be strengthening and corporate managerial autonomy at the regional level growing as firms adopt new forms of subcontracting, enter joint ventures, form strategic alliances and embed themselves more deeply in regional networks (Ohmae, 1993).

Regionalisation covers any of the processes by which regional autonomy is enhanced. Decision making is more regionalised when it enhances the autonomy of regional institutions *from* other levels of government or when autonomy *to* achieve a greater range of things is increased. In other words, one refers primarily to politico-administrative discretion; the other is concerned with decision-making capacity. In a governmental sense, regionalisation can result from the decentralisation of powers, resources and responsibilities from the national level or from a form of centralisation when they are passed up from sub-regional or local level. But it can also be achieved through a third route: the creation of extra decision-making capacity. Whatever the route it takes, regionalisation describes the build-up of any of the resources mentioned above at regional level. It does not necessarily involve the creation or further empowerment of democratically elected regional governments. The creation of a regional development agency, for example, is a form of regionalisation even if it is not accountable to regional government. Firms, as well as governments, can regionalise decision making, for example by developing 'flatter' hierarchies and decentralised budget centres.

On these criteria, UK regions have traditionally been administratively unimportant except where the relevant boundaries are also national ones. Regionalism is variable but weakly developed overall. Regionalist and nationalist sentiments combine much more powerfully in the non-English nations than elsewhere. Regional autonomy is weak but variable; the stateless nations have the highest level of discretion. Regionalisation has been a response to nationalist pressures but it has also been characterised by administrative deconcentration from the centre, designed to improve policy implementation and coordination and address regional inequalities.

The research and the structure of the report

In order to make sense of pressures for regionalisation and to relate them to the key questions outlined above, the research programme undertook two main tasks. First, it examined the extent and form of recent regionalisation in the UK across a range of policy sectors to determine whether any broad pattern could be discerned. The research involved an audit of major regional organisations and structures created within the last decade or so. It compared their basic features, such as organisational status, function, rationale, boundary of operation, degree of autonomy and shifts in the balance of power between national, regional and local tiers. The results of the audit are presented in Chapter 2. Fuller details are set out in Appendix 1.

Secondly, the programme focused on the policy field most relevant to arguments about the relation between regional institutional capacity and economic dynamism – economic development. Here, a case study approach was adopted. The choice of regions to study was based on two criteria. First, it reflected a wish to limit the variation in economic fortunes so that like could be compared with like. Secondly, it maximised the degree of institutional variation to understand how this might affect regional capacity to respond to common economic changes. The research covered Scotland, Wales, the North East and the North West because these 'regions' suffered acutely from structural economic adjustment. But they also offer very strong UK contrasts in governing structures and institutional capacity for economic development.

The research rejected a highly economistic analysis which could have provided statistical rankings of institutional performance but would have seen the institutional framework itself simply as a black box which turns inputs into outputs. Instead, it concentrated upon how the black box works – upon 'how' and 'why' rather than 'what' questions. The case studies looked at the way regional economic prospects and potentials were perceived, how these perceptions informed strategic responses, and how widely they were shared. They examined the regional institutional structures that affected policy success, how regional institutions related to each other on economic matters and what part regional coherence, consciousness and solidarity played in interorganisational networking. The research drew upon the perceptions of those actors, agencies and interests most closely involved in promoting regional economic development. Chapters 3 and 4 compare and contrast the experiences of the case study regions.

The final chapter returns to the key questions with which this chapter started. It asks how persuasive are the arguments that regional government in the UK could (i) be based on the democratisation of current regional agencies and policy delivery, and (ii) produce better regional economic performance. In suggesting answers to these questions, it looks briefly at trends in other European countries and assesses a number of alternative principles of reform which might be considered for UK circumstances.

Notes

1 Unless readers know better, we credit this phrase to James Mitchell of the Government Department, Strathclyde University.

Chapter 2

The regionalisation of policy making

Regionalisation described

Just as systems of regional administration differ, so recent regionalisation trends have not been uniform across the UK. In Scotland and Wales, as one of the project's interviewees expressed it, a 'salami slice' of Whitehall responsibility has been passed to the Scottish and Welsh Offices each year since the last election. The biggest departure from the pre-1992 situation, however, has been in England. Since this report is concerned primarily with degrees of change in regional decision making, this chapter inevitably deals mostly with the English experience. Here, the bulk of recent additional regional activity has been caused by the creation of quangos, or 'non-departmental public bodies'. Far from breaking with the past, this trend continues a non-executive tradition of English regional administration on the part of central government. The diversity in the status, functions and boundaries of operation of recently created regional organisations and structures does not suggest that a single, coherent regional tier of governance is emerging. Indeed, as Table 1 indicates, there are at least ten different types of regional body:

- deconcentrated, interdepartmental offices of central government departments, the new Government Offices for the Regions (GORs);

- the regional offices of single central government departments, for example the Department of Health's Social Services Inspectorate (SSI), the Office of Standards in Education (Ofsted);

- quangos and executive agencies with regional offices, for example the Housing Corporation or Next Steps Agencies such as the Highways Agency;

- government departments or quangos whose head offices are internally structured on a regional basis, for example the Funding Agency for Schools;

- free-standing, nominally private organisations which operate within an overall framework agreed with their national equivalents and which depend upon central government grant, for example Regional Arts Boards;

- joint regional authorities in metropolitan areas, created after the abolition of the Greater London Council and the metropolitan county councils, overseen by councillors appointed by district and borough authorities and responsible for fire and civil defence, police, waste disposal;
- umbrella organisations formed by local bodies to articulate common regional interests, for example English Regional Associations of local authorities;
- bodies which are also supported by central government to provide a jointly agreed, strategic, contextual statement to underpin regional actions, for example Regional Planning Conferences;
- private regional utility companies, for example regional water and electricity companies;
- regional advisory committees of the utilities' regulatory bodies – the Offices of Water Services (Ofwat), Gas Services (Ofgas), Electricity Regulation (Offer) and the National Rivers Association (NRA).

In most other policy sectors there has been substantial continuity and few demands for the regional administration of services. Many functions, particularly those in the fields of social, cultural, leisure, transport, environmental and refuse services and development control, are still administered by local authorities. There has been little change, either, in the handling of functions where a more strategic perspective is required, for example, the joint boards established to handle strategic functions after the abolition of the English metropolitan authorities.

The rationale for increased regional administration

Increased regional activity stems either from variations upon familiar themes in central–local government relations or from the administrative demands of new modes of governance. Regional offices and regional internal structures of central government departments, agencies and quangos are hardly new. They reflect a long-standing division of functions whereby national government controls policy objectives, expenditure and service levels whilst implementation is handled at sub-national level to allow for the diversity of local and regional circumstances, the tapping of local intelligence and liaison between local organisations. In other words, they are established primarily for administrative convenience. As a result, there is nothing sacrosanct about regional institutions and their forms tend to change much more frequently than do those of elected agencies. Regional Health Authorities (RHAs), for example, have recently been amalgamated to achieve savings in overheads. Government policy has nonetheless led to a growth in regional governmental activity, if sometimes inadvertently, for five main reasons:

Regulating the market

When the utilities were privatised, the government established regulatory bodies to protect consumer interests. These are structured along regional lines not only to shadow regionally based utility companies but also to prevent operators from abusing their monopolistic powers in local segments of the supply network. Similarly, in health, RHAs have assumed new roles in managing local 'quasi-markets' created as a result of the separation of purchasing and providing in health care. RHAs provide a regional overview of investment needs, specify performance targets, handle cross-boundary issues and balance the interests of stakeholders – providers, purchasers and professional interests.

Cost savings and quality

Central government's need to monitor the performance of sub-national government has grown as pressures to reduce public expenditure, whilst maintaining or raising the quality of services, have intensified. This has spawned regional inspectorates whose functions are to check that local organisations comply with national performance targets, for example, in the Citizen's Charter. Government expenditure cuts have also encouraged 'government by contract' where goals, targets and resource levels are set centrally but detailed, often painful, funding priorities are decided at regional level. Ostensibly, this system improves the prospects of attracting contributions from other regional partners and ensures that rationing decisions are taken in the light of local knowledge. An alternative interpretation, however, is that in some sectors such as tourism and arts, whilst a contract-based system promises more autonomy *from* the centre, autonomy *to* achieve things is limited by cuts in overall resources, tight contract-based financial controls, and strict performance targets.

Table 1: The nature of recently established regional bodies

Regional organisation (date established)	Status	Type of region (no.; boundary)	Degree of autonomy	Change in distribution of power
Government Regional Offices (1993)	Government departments (DOE, DTI, DE, DT)	Administrative (10 approx. standard regions)	Moderate	=
English Partnerships regional offices (1993)	Quango	Administrative (6 own)	Moderate	=
English Regional Associations, Regional Planning Conferences (by 1992)	Voluntary association of LA's	Administrative (9 standard regions)	Minimal	=
Water Companies and OFWAT (1989/90); Regional electricity companies and OFFER (1990/1)	Private companies and quangos	Operational	Significant, regulators less so	+ water - electricity
Regional Offices of Housing Corporation (1964) - 2 new Regional Offices in SE (1995)	Quango	Administrative (10 approx. std. regions)	Moderate	=
Fire and Civil Defence Authorities (1986)	Joint Board	Metropolitan (6 counties)	Significant	=
Joint Police Authorities (1986)	Joint Authority	Metropolitan (6 counties)	Moderate	=
Regional Health Authorities (1994)	Quangos	Administrative (8 own)	Moderate	=
Social Services Inspectorate (1992)	Government department (DH)	Administrative (4-6 own)	Minimal	=
Further Educational Funding Council - regional offices (1992)	Quango	Administrative (9 regions)	Minimal	+
Office for Standards in Education - regional offices (1992)	Non-Ministerial government department	Administrative (14 own)	Minimal	=
Funding Agency for Schools - regional structure (1994)	Quango	Administrative (6 own)	Moderate	+

Regional organisation (date established)	Status	Type of region (no.; boundary)	Degree of autonomy	Change in distribution of power
Next Steps Agencies with provincial offices (since 1988)	Executive Agencies of Central Govt.	Operational (various)	Moderate	=
Regional Arts Boards (1991)	Independent limited companies	Administrative (10 approx. standard regions)	Moderate	-
Regional Tourist Boards (1969)	Quangos	Administrative (11 approx. standard regions)	Moderate	-
Regional Councils of Sport and Recreation (1960s)	Royal charter	Administrative (aggregations of counties)	Moderate	=

= straight increase in regional capacity
+ regionalisation (powers passed up)
- regionalisation (powers passed down)

Replacing local government

The steady removal of functions and powers from local authorities has created a void which quangos have attempted to fill by organising themselves on a territorial basis to ensure the continuation of local authorities' expertise and their accessibility to the public and to sectoral interests. The Further Education Funding Council, where regional rather than local arrangements have been adopted to reap economies of scale and minimise overheads, is a clear example of this.

Regional integration and partnership

The proliferation of quangos and the multiplicity of urban regeneration and area-based economic development initiatives have created widespread concern about fragmentation and duplication. The government has responded to calls for better policy coordination and coherence in its activities by consolidating those departments with regional offices into regional 'one-stop-shops'. Government has also recast some regionally structured quangos like English Partnerships and the Regional Tourism Boards to act in an enabling role, using government money to weld together local partnerships. Recognition by government of the need for locally informed strategic planning guidance at the regional level to be incorporated into structure plans to minimise land use conflicts and overcome 'nimbyism' has been a further response to local institutional fragmentation.

Reaction to excessive central bureaucracy

In some policy spheres there is growing consensus that the centralisation of power and the bureaucracy it generates has stifled local initiative. For example, Regional Arts Boards have been granted greater formal independence and funding responsibility to take more account of local judgement and knowledge in funding decisions, to encourage flexibility and innovation and to dovetail activities with those of other important local funding agencies, principally local authorities.

The reasons for increased regional administrative activity have been extremely varied. In some cases it has happened as much by default as by design. Underlying this messy pattern, however, the traditional centrist argument for a regional tier of *administration* – that it suits central government's convenience in providing 'hands off' implementation, but within acceptable degrees of discretion – prevails over those which argue the need for more regional autonomy from the centre. As ever, central government derives a range of benefits from regional administration. These include its ability to

- mediate between central requirements and local needs;
- relieve the centre of administrative detail;
- offer local accessibility;
- cushion the centre from the impact of its expenditure decisions;
- add legitimacy by adapting central directives to regional circumstances;
- provide strategic context;
- achieve regional economies of scale.

Boundary definition and coherence

One test of the coherence of regionalisation is the degree of fit between the boundaries of different regional organisations or national organisations with regional structures. In England, whilst most regional entities cover areas that approximate to the standard regions, there is significant variation in the precise boundaries adopted in different policy sectors. In most cases, England has been divided up into between 8 and 12 provincial regions of roughly similar size for administrative convenience. Quangos and other nationally-inspired bodies are usually structured on this basis. Scotland and Wales are invariably administered as separate entities, although in some cases there are also sub-regional offices. In other cases, boundaries reflect the operational and functional requirements of delivering particular services. Finally, some services are delivered on a metropolitan scale as a compromise between maintaining local accountability and identity whilst reaping economies of scale on one hand and exploiting interdependencies between land use and transportation planning on the other.

Even within these broad headings, however, there is still substantial variation, since:

- most boundaries were originally defined according to narrow functional requirements and irrespective of whether the parts they produced could ever add up to a regional whole;
- the precise criteria for boundary definition vary and include operational efficiency (police and fire), cultural identity (arts), volume of case burden (SSIs, Ofsted), territorial range of local organisations (Housing Corporation regional offices) and size,

similarity of character and indigenous institutional culture (Further Education Funding Council);

- continuity and inertia militate against all forms of change, especially when the current system appears to be working tolerably well.

There has, however, been some recent evidence of convergence. For example:

- better integrated financial planning in the housing sector has resulted in the Housing Corporation realigning its boundaries to more closely match those of the GORs;

- the Further Education Funding Council (FEFC) has adopted the same boundaries as the GORs (with the exception of Merseyside) to integrate the education and training components of regional economic development plans and labour market assessments.

These examples suggest that the development of the GORs in England may prompt a move toward common and coherent boundary definitions by other agencies. In other words, they might encourage regional institutionalisation in the same way as has long been the case in Scotland and Wales. Once again, though, the signs do not all point in the same direction. Some new agencies continue to adopt different boundaries – English Partnerships is a case in point. Similarly, the case for standardisation amongst existing agencies undergoing reform is often outweighed by the logic of continuing to use the boundaries of predecessor organisations to maintain continuity and limit the costs of reorganisation. In other cases, the scope for reducing property overheads and staffing through amalgamation has overridden other factors. The road to common regional boundaries is likely to be long and winding as departmental and operational criteria compete with, and sometimes cut across, territorial considerations.

Degrees of regional autonomy

A key issue for this study was whether the growth in governmental activity at regional level had been accompanied by greater regional autonomy overall. The answer that emerged from the audit was that it had not. At one end of the spectrum, regional organisations are administrative, inspecting or information-gathering arms of central government. In other words, there is limited autonomy *from* higher levels of government. At the other end, the very limited control over finances and policy making wielded by some regional bodies is offset by considerable devolution of management responsibility and discretion over the means of implementation. In short, autonomy *to* achieve

Conclusion

Many of the new regional organisations are quangos which appear powerful locally and attract criticism for their ability to deploy resources without requiring local consent. In reality, however, they are rather like Gulliver in Lilliput, held down by a multitude of central controls, targets, operating guidelines and ministerial reserve powers. The most significant power at regional level now rests in the hands of the Senior Regional Director of the Government Offices. But even here regional power is limited by the respective central departments and the fact that GORs are only responsible for around 10% of government expenditure in each region.

However, in some sectors the changes have not all been one way. Despite continued centralisation of control, there has been greater devolution of managerial responsibility within quangos and government departments. This runs counter to traditional tendencies to deconcentrate mainly administrative functions. The pressure to raise performance and quality, for example, by complying with the Citizen's Charter and other targets, despite limited resources, accounts for responsibilities being pushed down to an operational level and to relatively junior field staff. Most key policies and targets are nonetheless still set centrally, not regionally or locally.

More responsibilities have passed upwards to regional level than downwards from central government, mainly because of the significant transfer of functions from local authorities to quangos and utility regulators. The government's claimed devolution from the centre has mainly consisted of the consolidation of government departments within the GORs, the transfer of powers from local education authorities to school governors and the creation of a system where budget holders amongst general practitioners and the district health authorities purchase health care in an internal market. It is not clear why the one-stop-shop idea necessarily entails a shift of power from the centre to GORs. The one explanation would seem to be that the government has reinterpreted devolution to mean only the pushing of purchasing responsibility down to the lowest operational level.

Whilst the evidence points to an overall process of centralisation, it is impossible to make blanket generalisations about all sectors. In economic development and strategic planning and to a lesser extent in the arts, tourism and leisure, there has not merely been growth in the volume of regional activity. Here, at least, there are signs that regional institutional capacity and coherence are growing in response to representations from private and public interests who increasingly want supportive governance with the discretion to fashion innovative and locally appropriate strategies to help unlock regional and national competitive potential. In the longer term, alliances between regionally-based utility companies and other economic development bodies may add to such demands. Greater institutional coherence, capacity and consistency in boundary definition has already made groupings of regional interests more willing to speak up and lobby on regional issues such as the need for coordinated infrastructural planning. Creation of GORs and increased adoption of the partnership philosophy by, for example, English Partnerships and RABs is promoting greater regional networking and policy making. Recent institutional developments at the regional level could therefore, despite much recent evidence to the contrary, herald more extensive changes in regional governance and hence the nature of central–local relations in the future.

Chapter 3

Regional economies and regional institutions

The case studies

This chapter and Chapter 4 test some key issues concerning the link between regional institutional capacity and performance and economic competitiveness. Assessing the added economic value of institutions and inter-agency networking is extremely complicated. Concepts like 'institutional thickness' (Amin and Thrift, 1994) have been coined to suggest that the density and pro-activity of local institutions and their interactions play an increasingly important role in helping localities adapt to globalising economic circumstances. How they do this, however, remains something of a mystery. What happens through luck, by design or as an unintended consequence of other deliberate decisions is difficult to determine. It is clear, though, that research needs to concern itself primarily with what *can* happen by design.

This project used a case study approach to test some simple propositions about the process. The basic assumption was that regions respond to economic change through thousands of small scale market adjustments, each of which has its own logic. But for a region to respond in an effective, coherent and proactive manner, there needs to be a clear understanding of the problems and potential of the region and its sub-areas and sectors. It requires a commitment to, and a means for, developing this understanding into a strategy for the region. That strategy might operate informally rather than formally. But it would be understood and endorsed by the major institutions along with key players in non-statutory sectors. There would be sufficient institutional capacity to deliver the strategy, major programmes and projects, including specialist agencies in economic development. The network of regional interests and institutions would also be able to mobilise external support, from inward investors and higher levels of government. One would also expect evidence of regional consciousness and solidarity linking key players and enabling effective interorganisational networking.

There is clearly enormous variation between UK regions in terms of these characteristics and it is possible to learn a number of lessons by comparing and contrasting their experiences. England's North East and

North West plus Scotland and Wales were chosen as case studies for this project precisely because of the contrasts in their institutional structures and in their distinctive regional or national identities. Much of the evidence relevant to the above propositions depends more upon judgement than on precise measurement. The core data for this section, therefore, were the perceptions of leading actors, agencies and interests involved in economic development issues.

Four 'regional economies'

There are a number of similarities between the economic fortunes of the four case study areas. Each of the four regions experiences European peripherality, lagging economic performance, low rates of innovation in traditional sectors, increasing external ownership, poor communications, pockets of high unemployment and environmental dereliction. Because economic linkages do not respect national or regional boundaries, and since each region is heavily wired into external circuits of business, it is difficult to speak of separate regional economies.

In Wales, for example, there are two sets of strong east–west linkages, between North Wales and Merseyside and between South Wales and the West Midlands and southern England. Transport infrastructures reinforce this pattern in that they help channel corporate linkages and patterns of inter-firm purchasing and supplies. In this way the economic prospects of Welsh firms are closely linked with neighbouring parts of England whilst north–south links between North and South Wales are comparatively undeveloped. Similar comments could be made about Scottish cross-border linkages and even more so about the English regions, where administrative borders have still less relevance for markets. Overall, the interdependency of UK regional economies and the similar experiences of sectoral change found in the four regions means that they are not strikingly different to each other or to the UK as a whole. That does not mean, though, that there are not different nuances.

Scotland

Broad sectoral and occupational changes in Scotland, for example, are similar to those of the UK generally (McCrone, 1993: ch 3). Scotland nonetheless has distinctive sectoral strengths, in: oil and oil-related industries; food, drink and tobacco, especially whisky; electrical and instrument engineering, particularly the largely foreign-owned electronics sector; financial services, especially in banking, fund management and life assurance, where key firms are still Scottish-owned; educational, medical and health services, and energy/water supply, agriculture, forestry and fishing, reflecting Scotland's rich natural resources (Scottish Office, 1994; Aitken, 1992). Scotland's small population size (5m) and limited domestic market means its prosperity has long rested upon the ability of home-based firms to trade beyond its borders. The resulting export orientation means that Scotland outstrips average UK performance in some respects. Scotland generates 8% of UK manufacturing output but 9.6% of exports, with computers and whisky being the biggest earners. Manufacturing productivity has also exceeded that of the UK in each of the last three decades, although it trails foreign competition by some way.

Since 1993 the unemployment rate in Scotland has been at or below the UK level for the first time since the war (see Figure 1). Given the recent, general levelling up of UK regional economic performance, however, this is cause for limited satisfaction. Despite its recent improvement, Scotland's lagging economic performance compared with more prosperous regions in the UK and beyond reflects a legacy of declining industries, principally steel, aluminium, shipbuilding, coal-mining, car production and heavy engineering. Failure to adjust to structural change more confidently and to effect a more decisive economic transition, it is argued (Scottish Enterprise, 1995), is the result of a number of factors:

- a relatively undemanding domestic market;
- low rates of new firm formation;
- cautious attitudes to risk by the major institutions;
- modest levels of product and process innovation, company research and development and business–higher education linkage;
- weak links between foreign-owned companies and Scottish suppliers;
- low levels of in-service training;
- a culture which does not promote or value entrepreneurialism.

Wales

The economic base in Wales has also undergone dramatic and painful transformations, with jobs in coal and slate mining, iron and steel and agriculture halving within a generation. Only two of a peak-time 600 coal pits now survive, whilst steel-making capacity has been cut by 80% in the last decade. Economic indicators such as unemployment (Figure 1), GDP per capita (Figure 2) and average earnings (Figure 3) portray a growing gap between Welsh and UK prosperity in the 1970s and 1980s. As in Scotland, though, in the last decade there have been positive signs of diversification. Wales has become attractive to inward investment from the US and Japan in new manufacturing industries, particularly in automotive and consumer electrical sectors (Figure 4). Developments in tourism and modern extractive industries have also counteracted rural decline.

As a result of this and the recent economic turn-down in southern regions of England, unemployment rates in Wales and the UK have recently converged (see Figure 1) and differences in the rate of regional employment change have narrowed. Heavy capital investment by new firms and low unit wage costs have markedly improved Welsh labour productivity, output and profitability. Since 1990, growth in manufacturing output and GDP in Wales has increasingly exceeded the national average (see Figure 5). Such growth is from a comparatively small base, however. Extremely low overall GDP per capita figures (see Figure 2) and low average disposable incomes per head (see Figure 3) remain major concerns. This reflects low wages within the newer firms compared with those in older heavy and extractive industries and Wales' relatively low profile in the highly-paid banking and financial service employment sector, which has boosted regional GDP and earnings in more prosperous regions.

The North East

There are many parallels between Wales and the North East in terms of population size – around 3m each – and the decline of traditional extractive and heavy industries, although the North East's list of industrial casualties also includes shipbuilding and chemicals. But the North East's decline from being one of the wealthiest industrial centres in the UK has been more dramatic. A third of the region's capacity in manufacturing, construction and primary sectors was lost in the early 1980s and regional GDP per capita fell from 94.3% of the UK average to 90.5% between 1981 and 1991. This reemphasised the region's consistent, comparative under-performance in terms of GDP (Figure 2), unemployment (Figure 1) and business survival rates since the war. This has stemmed from over-dependence upon declining industries and markets, a lack of diversification in traditional manufacturing activities, comparatively slow growth of service employment, dependence upon large, externally-owned firms (80% and rising), the related weakness of local entrepreneurialism and innovation, peripherality and the comparative lack of research and development and other higher order functions such as company headquarters.

Public sector trends in privatisation, deregulation, expenditure reduction and marketisation have also hit the region hard because of the high proportion of regional jobs in government services. The flight of financial services, especially from Newcastle to Leeds, is a further problem. As a result, service sector activity has grown more slowly than nationally. But its significance in employment terms, especially in health and education, is increasing. Overall, manufacturing remains strategically important to the regional economy, employing 21.5% of the workforce compared with 18.5% nationally and accounting for over 30% of regional output (Figure 5). Its high export content supports many other jobs. Bulk chemicals, pharmaceuticals, offshore fabrication, food and drink, engineering and to a lesser extent textiles remain key sectors. The North East has benefited, albeit less than Scotland and Wales, from substantial inward investment in automobiles and consumer electronics, mainly from Japan but also more recently from Korea, Taiwan and Germany (Figure 4). The region's attractiveness to inward investors is due to its abundant supply of cheap land, good port facilities, expanding higher educational institutions, manufacturing strengths and traditions, good industrial relations, low-cost labour and the cooperative attitude of regional economic development agencies.

The North West

The North West is the largest region outside London and the south east in terms of population and GDP. It is extremely diverse, economically and socially. The region's economic structure is broadly similar to the national picture. Surprisingly, it is not especially orientated towards manufacturing, its traditional strength and source of wealth. The region nonetheless has a continuing tradition of manufacturing with many large firms in engineering, energy, chemicals and pharmaceuticals (Figure 5). Its many higher education institutions give it a strong knowledge base. The region's sheer size means it can support highly specialised business functions, training and education facilities and specialist firms and a range of local cultural, leisure and media functions. Manchester airport and the port of Liverpool are two major gateways to European and world markets and the internal transport network is reasonably efficient and developed.

The region nonetheless under-performs by national standards in terms of GDP, employment growth and business formation (Figure 2). Within the North West, areas like east Lancashire, parts of Cheshire, northern greater Manchester and Merseyside face particularly severe restructuring problems. They contain concentrations of sectors in defence-related industries, car manufacturing, clothing and footwear and the nuclear industry which are particularly vulnerable to changes in European and global markets or in public procurement patterns. Their problems underline the effect of the European single market in exacerbating the region's peripherality (Peck, 1993). Such problems are superimposed upon long-standing structural ones. Pockets of very high unemployment in the region's urban areas reflect past contraction of key sectors such as port and port-related industry in Liverpool and textiles in Manchester and the smaller Lancashire towns. Together, these have left a poor quality physical environment across the region's central urban industrial belt. The fact that the North West has failed to match the success of Wales and the North East, far less Scotland, in attracting inward investment is a key strategic concern (Figure 4).

Summary

Figure 6 confirms that the differences between the case study regions are essentially matters of degree. In terms of population and employment levels, GDP, number of firms and earnings, all travelled on a downward trajectory relative to the national average between 1981-91. Wales was the only partial exception to this general trend, experiencing a modest increase in population and GDP in the period. As Figure 7 shows, however, the pattern has changed since 1991. Scottish and Welsh unemployment rates have converged with the national average. And all four regions experienced modest improvements in their relative position in GDP and earnings. This stems from limited improvements in the four regions' economic performance but, more important, the down-turns in the service-dominated economies of more prosperous regions during the most recent recession. Impressive GDP growth in Scotland, Wales and the North East from 1991-93 appears to be linked to the performance of foreign-owned firms since the GDP figure for the North West, the least successful of the four regions in attracting inward investment, is only slightly above the national average.

Figure 1: Seasonally adjusted unemployment rates in the four regions and the UK (1979-95)

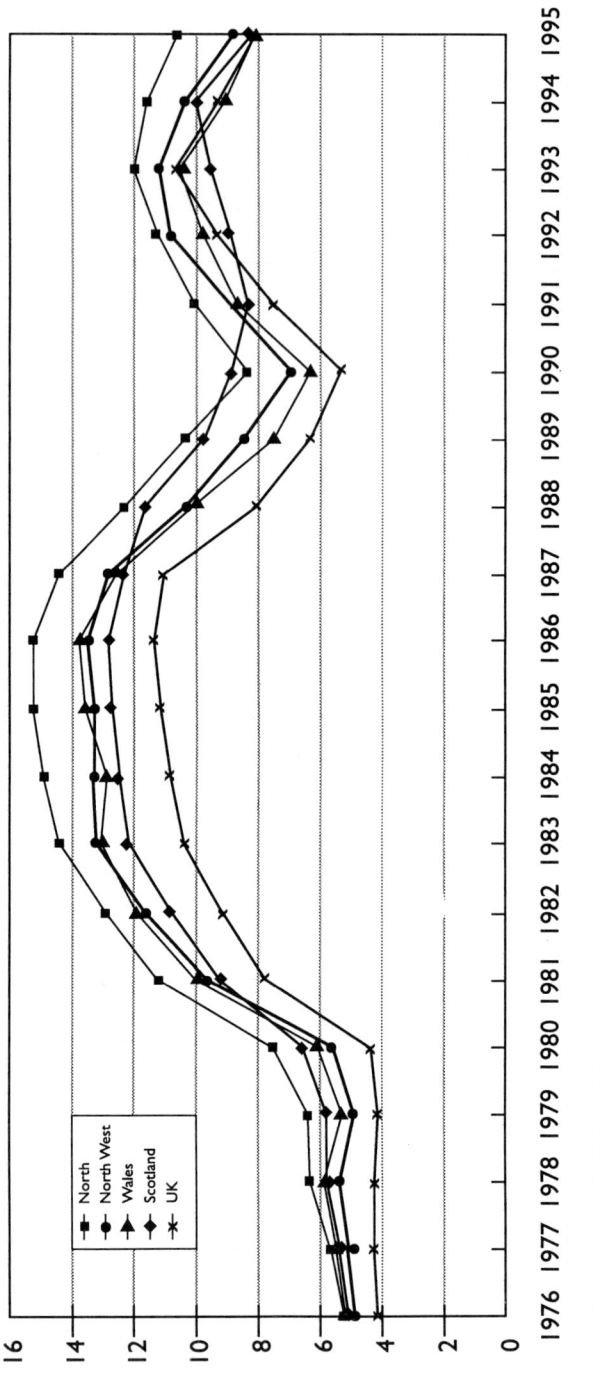

Source: *NOMIS*, 1995

Figure 2: GDP per capita in the four regions (1977-92) (UK = 100)

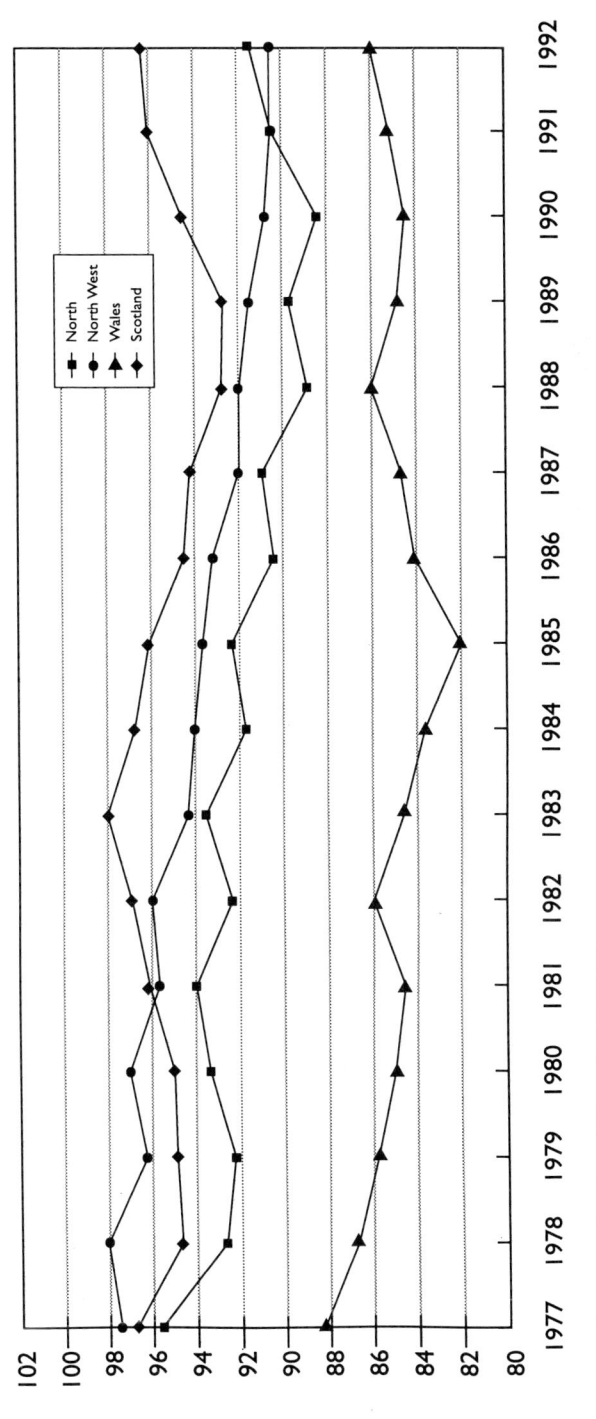

Source: *Regional Trends 1977-92*

Figure 3: Average gross weekly earnings (full-time) in the four regions (1977-93) (GB = 100)

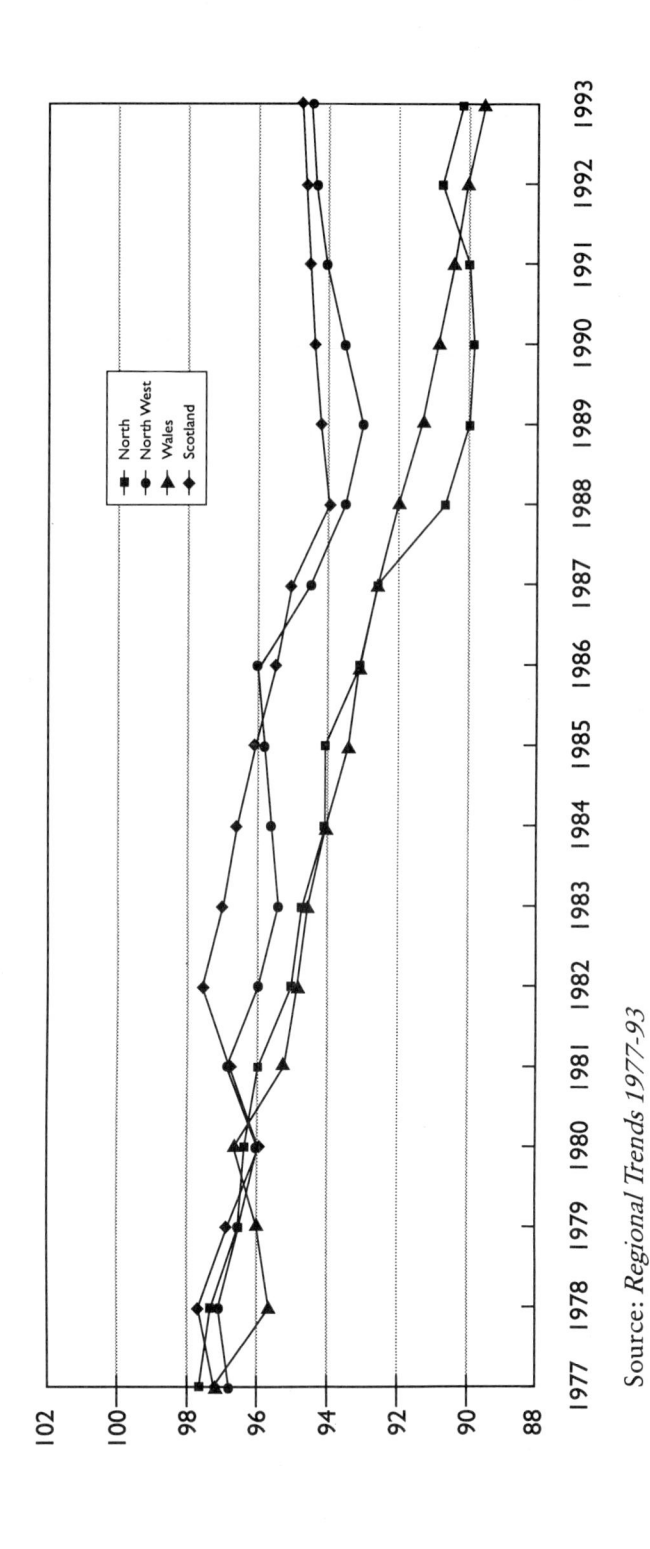

Source: *Regional Trends 1977-93*

Figure 4: Jobs created by foreign investment projects in the four regions (1983-95)

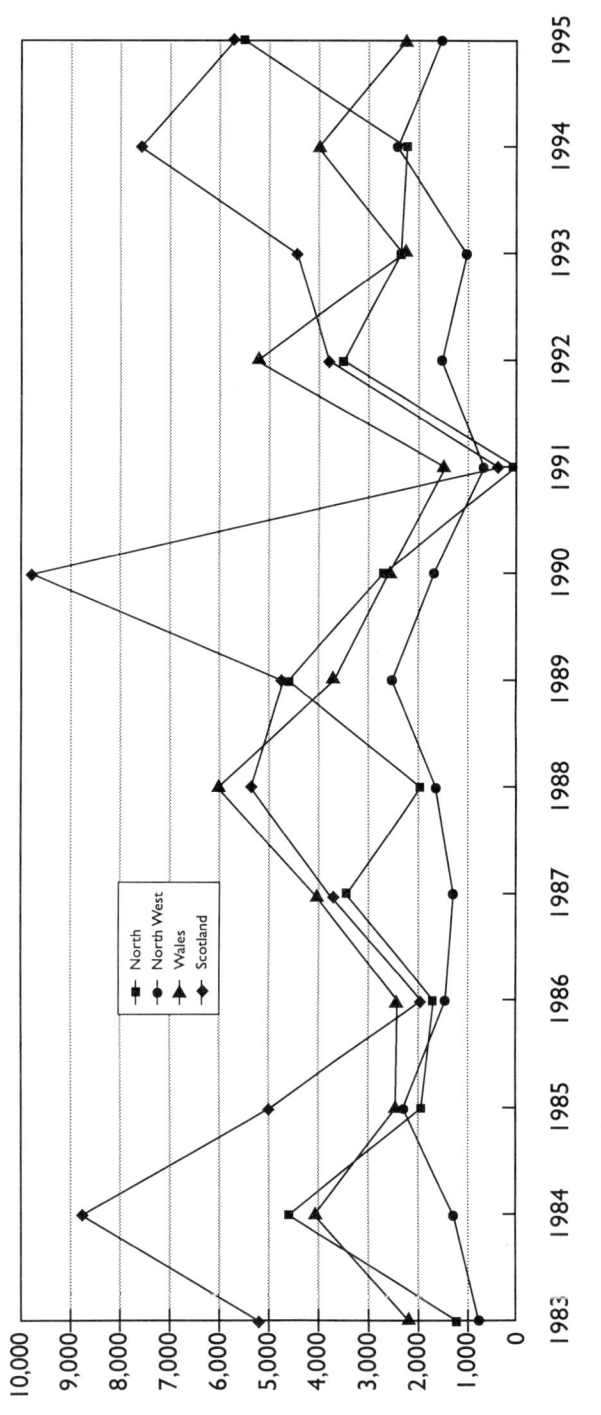

Source: *Regional Trends 1983-95*

Figure 5: Manufacturing GDP in the four regions and the UK (1977-92) (% of total GDP)

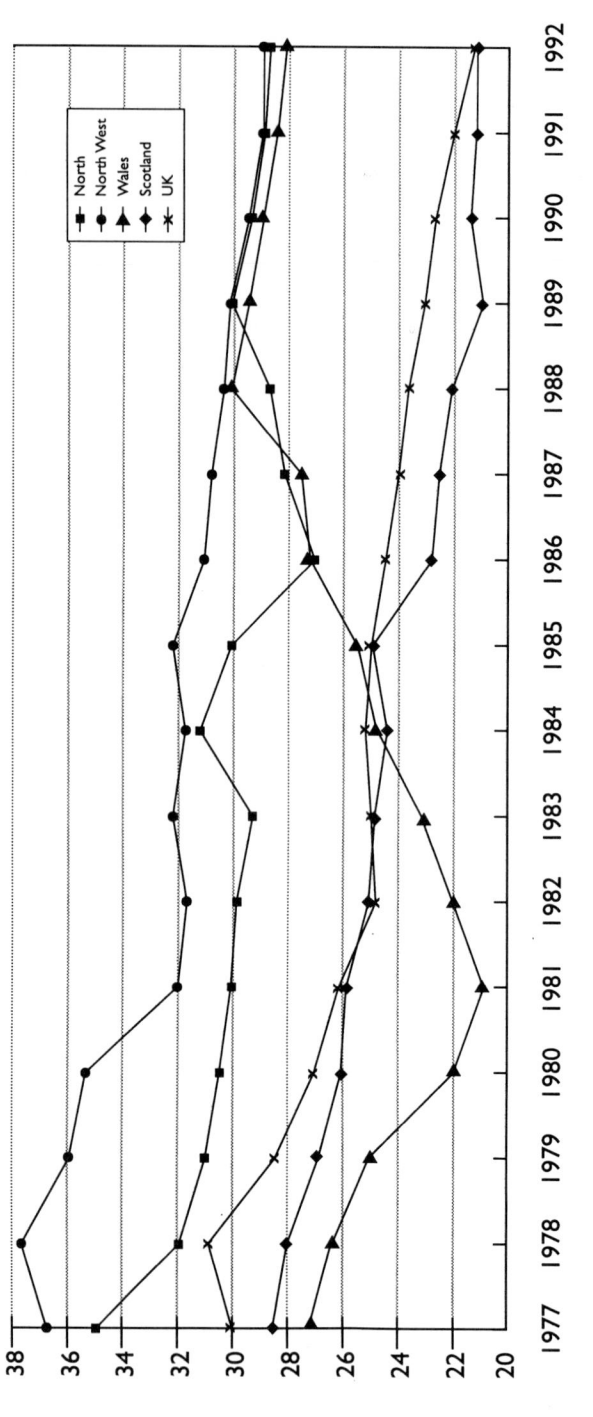

Source: *Regional Trends 1977-92*

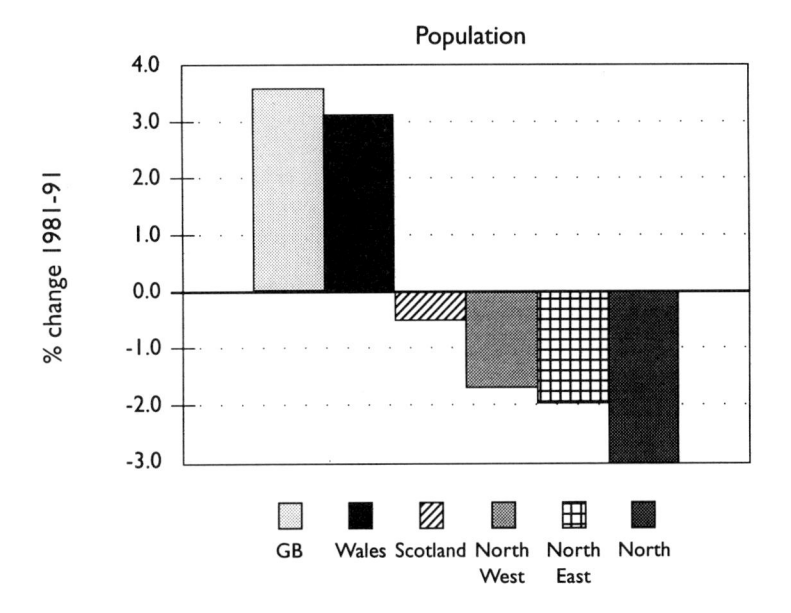

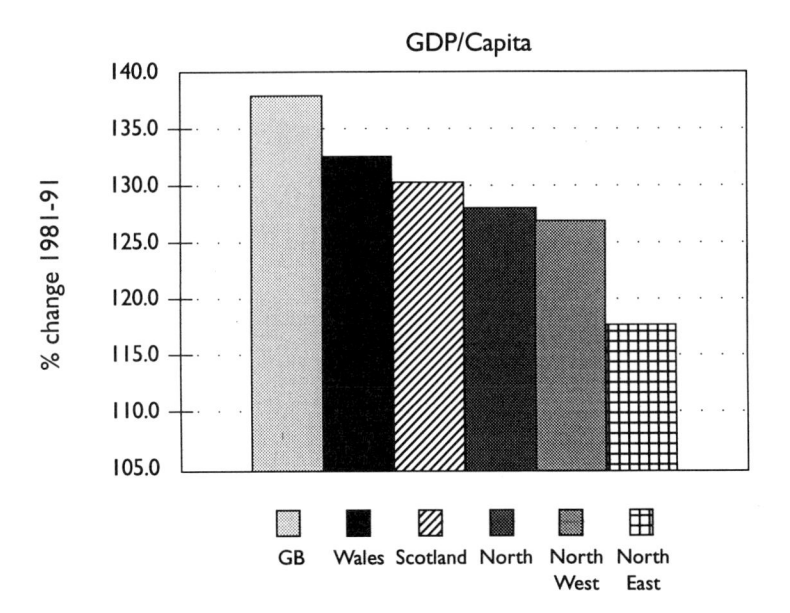

Figure 6: % change in selected indicators in the four regions and GB (1981-91)

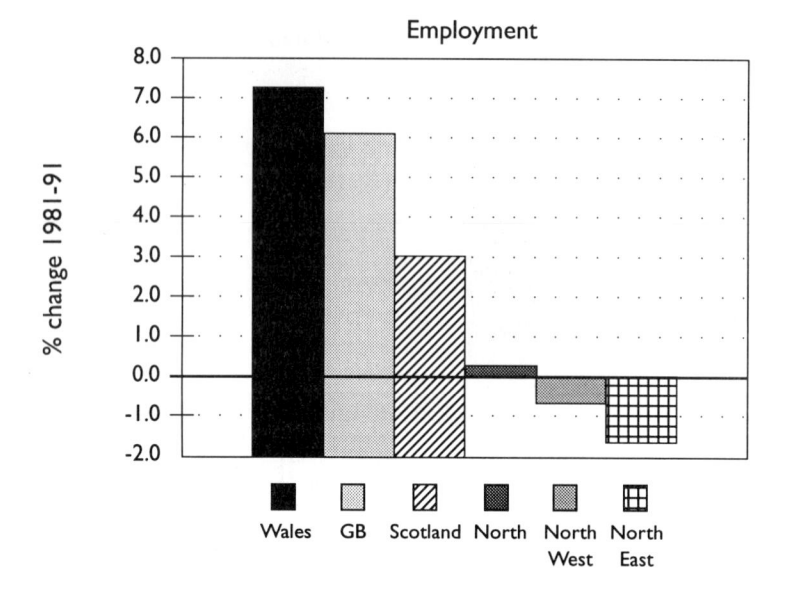

Employment

% change 1981-91

Region	% change
Wales	7.2
GB	6.1
Scotland	3.0
North	0.2
North West	-0.7
North East	-1.6

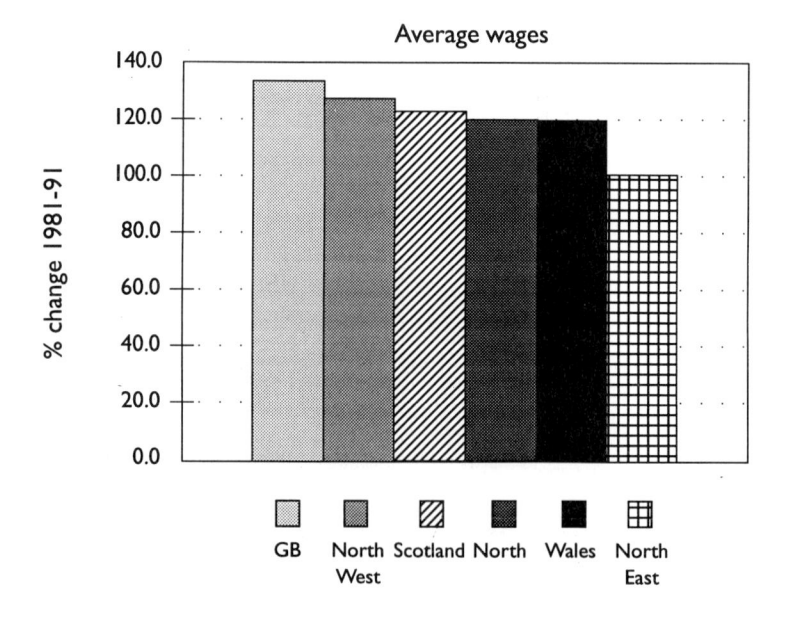

Average wages

% change 1981-91

Region	% change
GB	133.0
North West	127.0
Scotland	122.0
North	119.0
Wales	118.0
North East	100.0

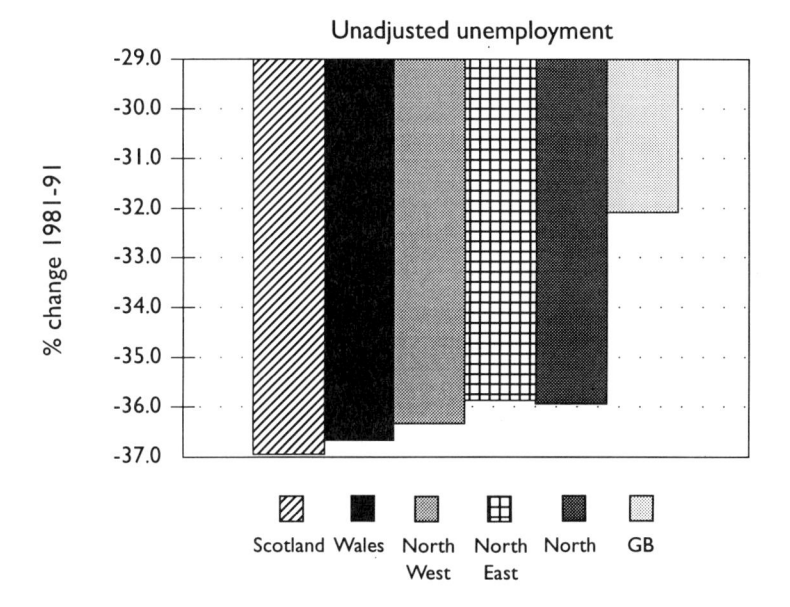

Unadjusted unemployment

% change 1981-91

Scotland, Wales, North West, North East, North, GB

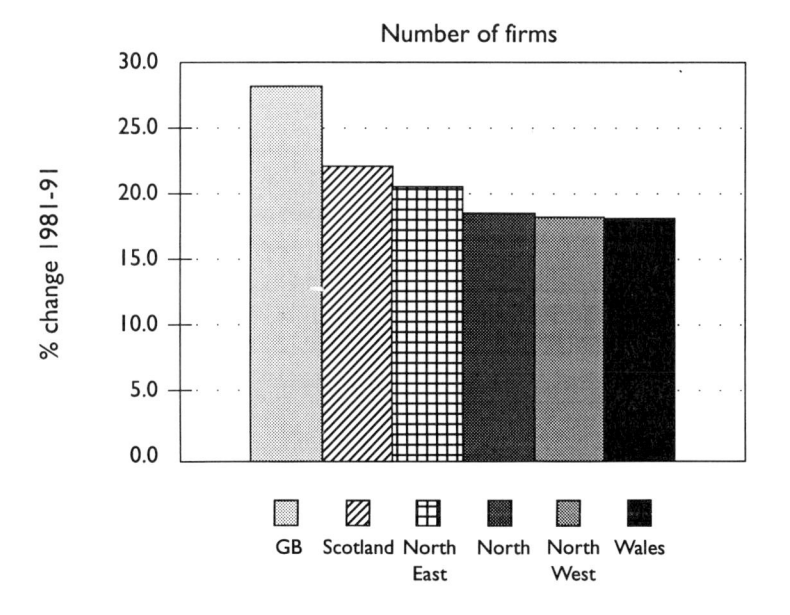

Number of firms

% change 1981-91

GB, Scotland, North East, North, North West, Wales

Figure 7: % change in selected indicators in the four regions and GB since 1991

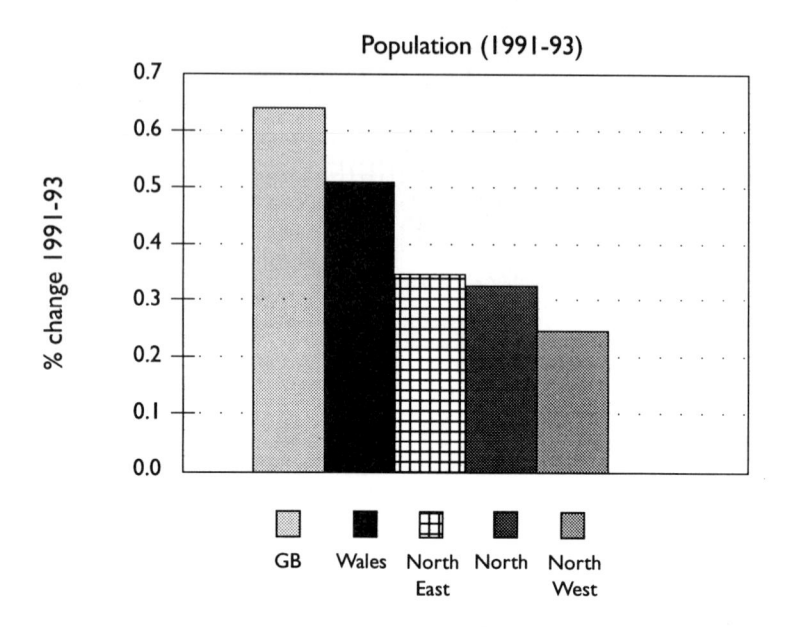

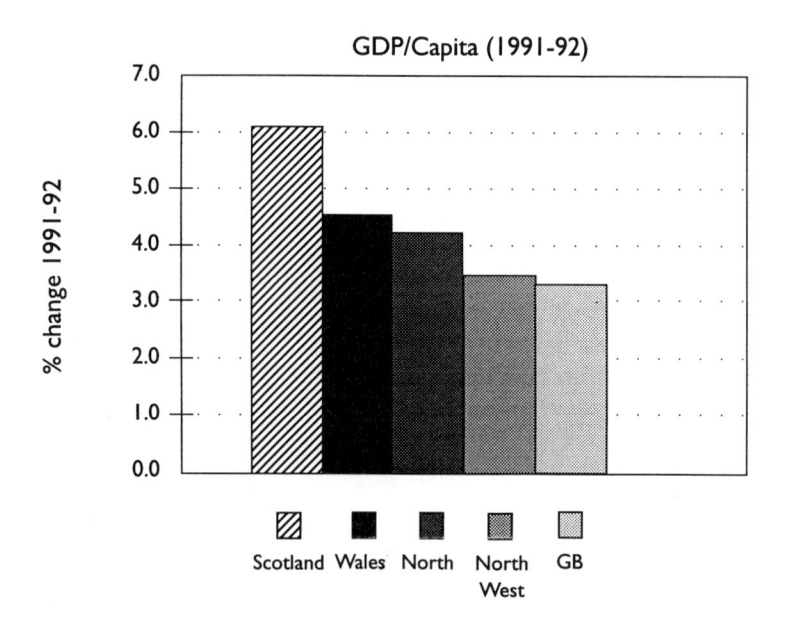

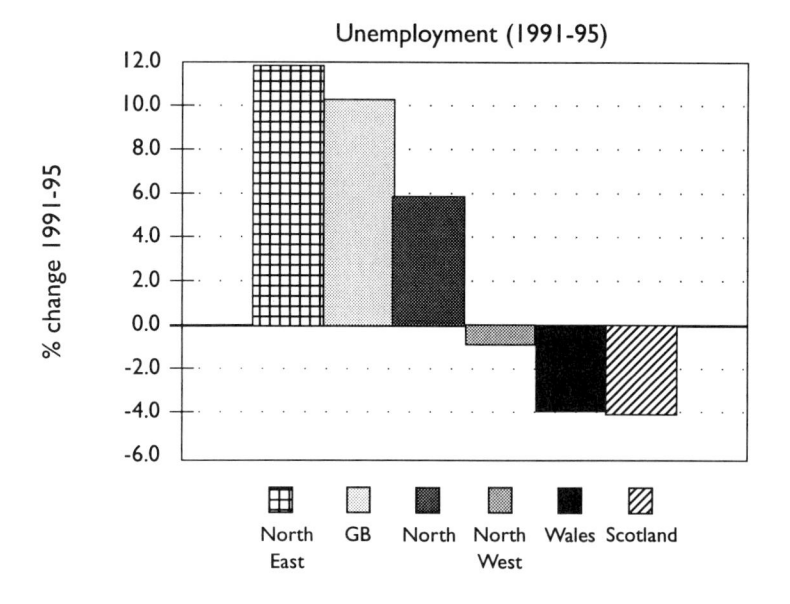

Unemployment (1991-95)

% change 1991-95

North East: ~11.8
GB: ~10.2
North: ~5.8
North West: ~-1.0
Wales: ~-4.0
Scotland: ~-4.2

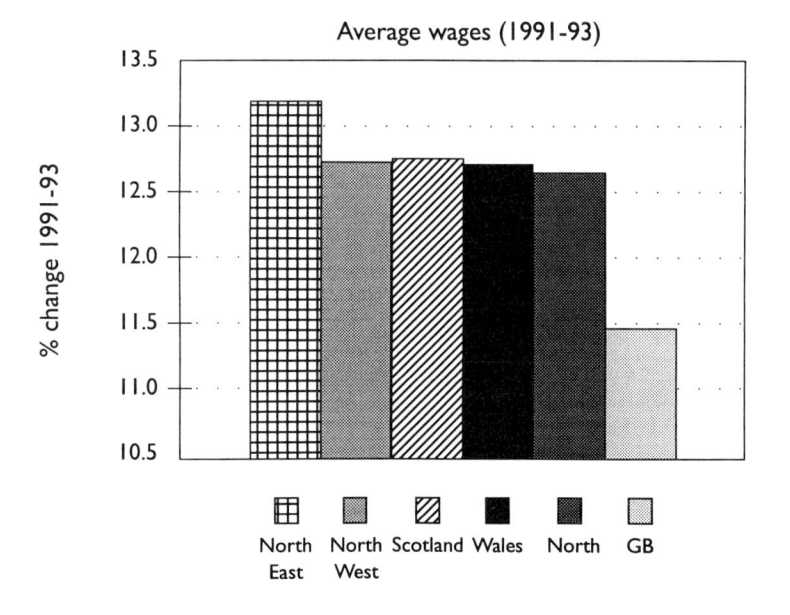

Average wages (1991-93)

% change 1991-93

North East: ~13.2
North West: ~12.7
Scotland: ~12.75
Wales: ~12.7
North: ~12.65
GB: ~11.45

Number of firms (1991-93)

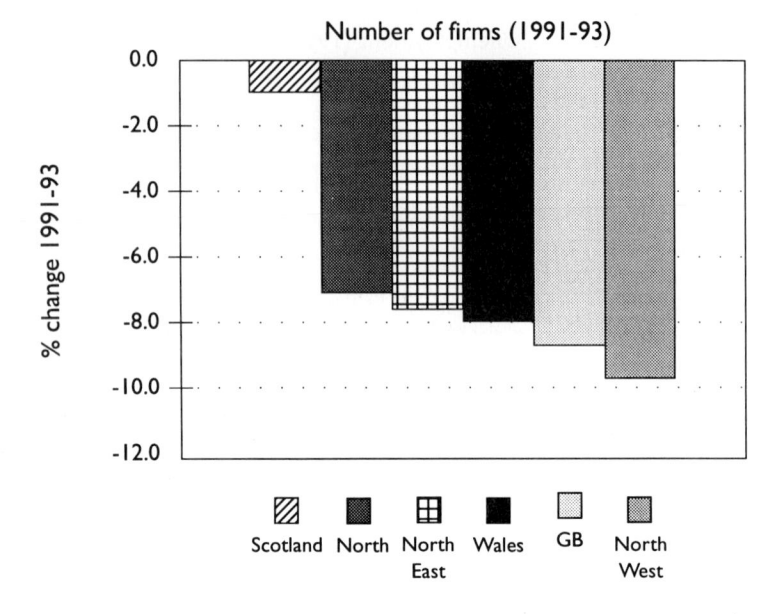

% change 1991-93 by region:
- Scotland: ~-1.0
- North: ~-7.0
- North East: ~-7.5
- Wales: ~-8.0
- GB: ~-8.7
- North West: ~-9.7

Institutional frameworks in the four regions

Despite their economic similarities, the four regions vary substantially in institutional terms. At one extreme lies Scotland. Strictly speaking, Scotland is a stateless nation, not a region, and its politics are strongly flavoured by nationalist, not just regionalist, sentiment (McCrone, 1993). Although part of the UK since 1707, it has always retained distinctive religious, legal and educational systems. As a result of a long but relatively peaceful struggle within the UK political system it also enjoys the most significant degree of *administrative* devolution of any sub-UK area (Kellas, 1975; Midwinter, Keating and Mitchell, 1991; Linklater and Denniston, 1992). Its key institution is the Scottish Office (SO) which is represented in Cabinet by a Scottish Secretary of State and contains four other government ministers. The SO enables the 'low politics' of Scotland to be largely decided upon and delivered by Scots whilst 'high politics' remains the preserve of Westminster and other Whitehall departments (Paterson, 1994).

Wales, too, has received special treatment on the grounds of similar, although less marked, nationalist sentiments and in the wake of institutional precedents set in Scotland. Most Welsh affairs are administered by the SO's territorial equivalent, the Welsh Office (WO), headed by the Welsh Secretary of State and containing two further Ministers. Formally, the WO is as powerful as its Scottish counterpart. But Wales' geographical proximity to England, and the fact that the WO has fewer staff with a less independent mentality, has meant that in practice it has tended to follow government policies much more straightforwardly.

The North East and North West lack these strong, territorially-rooted arms of government. But they also differ from each other. In terms of the government's regional presence, the North East is presided over by one integrated GOR, embracing former regional departments of environment, industry, employment and transport. By contrast, the North West has two GORs, one covering Merseyside and the other the remainder of the region. There is also a much keener sense of regional identity within the North East which, amongst other things, has produced a tradition of corporatist relations between public and private sectors, especially in the economic development sphere (Shaw, 1993). Despite continuing rivalry between the three conurbations of Tyneside, Wearside and Teesside, the North East is culturally and institutionally more integrated than the North West. There, regional institutions are thinner on the ground and of more recent origin. They struggle to demonstrate their legitimacy.

Table 2 summarises the main public and private institutions operating at regional level in each of the case study areas. The centre of the institutional web in Scotland is the SO. Proponents of a Scottish Parliament question the SO's ability to develop Scottish solutions to Scottish problems under current constitutional arrangements. However, the fact that critics rarely call for its reform, far less its abolition, suggests the SO has considerable capacity for relatively autonomous, delegated decision making compared with that available within the English regions. The SO's 6,000 staff, organised into five departments, have powers and responsibilities in the fields of agriculture and fisheries, education, training, environment, housing, local government, land-use planning, police, health, industry and economic development. The bulk of economic development responsibilities rest with the Industry and Environment Departments.

The SO's very existence makes it substantially easier to coordinate executive decision-making at the Scottish scale than is the case in the English regions, even allowing for GORs. Scotland also has a broader range of more powerful statutory and non-statutory economic development bodies. In the statutory field, two development agencies, Scottish Enterprise (SE) and Highlands and Islands Enterprise (HIE) coordinate a network of independently-constituted Local Enterprise Companies (LECs) whose boards comprise key non-statutory and public sector leaders. SE and HIE report to, and receive annual strategic guidance from, the SO's Employment and Industry Department (SOEID). They then prepare their own guidance for the LECs who contract to provide all services except those of Scottish-level strategic importance. These arrangements have a number of ostensible advantages over those, based on the more centralised Scottish Development Agency (SDA), that preceded them. They integrate economic development and labour market programmes. They are decentralised and therefore more sensitive to local needs and perspectives within a Scottish strategic framework. And they draw substantially upon private sector expertise and leadership (for discussion, see Scottish Select Committee, 1995; Fairley, 1990, 1992; Hayton, 1992).

SE and SOEID also jointly supervise two further, important economic development agencies. Locate in Scotland (LiS) was established in 1981 and has the best record in attracting inward investment of any agency in the UK. Scottish Trade International (STI) was set up recently to promote Scottish exports and international business links. Scotland also has a 'representative' office in Brussels which works independently from the UK government office. Scotland Europa, established in 1993, channels information from its sponsor organisations – SE, Scotland's local authority association (CoSLA) and the Scottish Trades Union Council (STUC) – to EU Directorates-General and undertakes contract work for private clients, including businesses (Mitchell, 1995).

Scotland's status as a nation also means that non-statutory institutions and interests are far more likely to operate Scotland-wide than at the level of an English region. Virtually every UK-wide professional or voluntary grouping has a Scottish equivalent. The autonomy of the Scottish element within such groupings varies. There is substantial ambiguity about, and tensions within and between, 'Scottish organisations' and those that are simply 'in Scotland'. The STUC, for example, clearly sees itself as a Scottish organisation. It remains independent of the UK TUC and represents affiliated unions on all Scottish-level matters. Similarly, CoSLA is the umbrella body for all Scottish local authorities and has substantial autonomy in conducting negotiations with the SO on their behalf. CBI Scotland, by contrast, has traditionally been the national CBI's regional office in Scotland. Only recently, since the national CBI has been encouraging regional offices to become more autonomous and involved in regional debates and issues, has CBI Scotland involved itself more deeply in Scottish campaigning and policy development (CBI Scotland, 1995).

In Wales, the WO and the two development agencies, the Welsh Development Agency (WDA) and the Development Board for Rural Wales (DBRW), have long dominated the economic development policy sphere. The agencies were originally established in the mid-1970s to provide a coherent, sustained and well-resourced strategic public response to Wales' severe economic problems. Since then, their importance and scope have grown. The WO has 2,000 staff and is responsible for 70% of all public expenditure in Wales. It has a department of Industry and Training, created in 1992 following the transfer of training functions from the Department of Employment, where most economic development responsibilities rest. Other departments oversee health, local government finance, planning and environment, transport and education. Although the WO has considerable scope to influence agency expenditure and policy content by framing operating criteria, it has not typically adapted national legislation and guidelines a great deal.

The Welsh Office's more passive policy stance reflects the fact that Welsh nationalism has tended to assume a cultural rather than economic form, as well as the absence of a significant Welsh corporate elite. However, recent highly-publicised controversies surrounding the two agencies has led to much closer WO scrutiny. The agencies' room for independent manoeuvre has also been constrained by expenditure cuts and modest transfers of resources to local authorities. Nonetheless, the WDA alone still receives almost as much grant-in-aid from the WO (£52m) as the 37 Welsh District Councils between them spend on economic development (£60-65m). The WDA continues to fulfil its original brief of working in close partnership with the private sector and others to further economic development, promote industrial efficiency and improve the environment. Its original concerns with land reclamation, factory-building and inward investment functions have been supplemented with a stress upon urban regeneration, the supplying of advanced business services and building links with dynamic areas of Europe.

Table 2: Principal institutions operating at the level of the case study regions

Institution	Scotland	Wales	North East	North West
Governmental	Scottish Office, Scottish Secretary, Four Ministers, Select Committee for Scottish Affairs, Scottish Grand Committee	Welsh Office, Welsh Secretary, Two Ministers, Select Committee for Welsh Affairs, Welsh Grand Committee	Government Office for the North East, Minister for NE	Two Government Offices (North West, Merseyside), Ministers for NW, Merseyside
Development Agencies	Scottish Enterprise, Highlands and Islands Enterprise	Welsh Development Agency, Development Board for Rural Wales, Land Authority for Wales	English Partnerships regional office	English Partnerships regional office
Inward investment and overseas trade agencies	Locate in Scotland, Scottish Trade International	(part of WDA)	Northern Development Company	INWARD
European lobby	Scotland Europa	Wales European Centre	Local Authority European offices	Local Authority European offices
Local authority representative bodies	Council of Scottish Local Authorities (COSLA)	Council for Welsh Districts, Assembly of Welsh Counties	North of England Assembly	North West Regional Association
Business representative bodies	CBI Scotland	CBI Wales	Northern CBI	North West CBI
	Scottish Chambers of Commerce, Scottish Business in the Community	Welsh Chamber of Commerce, Business in the Community Wales	North East Chamber of Commerce	North West Chambers of Commerce Association
Public/private partnership	Scottish Council (Development and Industry)		Northern Info. Applications Agency, Regional Technology Centre	North West Regional Partnership
Trades Unions	Scottish TUC	Welsh TUC	North East TUC	North West TUC
Private groupings	Scottish Electronics Forum	Institute of Welsh Affairs, Wales Engineering Centre	Manufacturing Challenge	North West Business Leadership Team
Private organisations	Scottish Financial Enterprise	Wales Quality Centre, World Trade Centre	Northern Offshore Federation (and other sectoral groupings)	NIMTECH (technology transfer)

DBRW's brief, paralleling that of HIE in parts of Scotland, is to promote the economic and social development of rural mid-Wales by diversifying areas over-dependent upon agriculture and tackling depopulation and the collapse of community services. It has constructed advance factories, attracted inward investment by aggressive marketing and promoting growth poles, undertaken initiatives in growth sectors and built up specialist knowledge in rural development. Other quangos, though less powerful, have also systematically addressed strategic weaknesses and opportunities in the Welsh economy. The work of the Welsh Tourist Board (WTB) is crucial to diversification, especially in rural areas. The Land Authority for Wales (LAW) has addressed the national shortage of development land attractive to developers by assembling sites in a strategic way.

As in Scotland, the concentration of devolved executive powers and functions has bred further institutionalisation at the all-Wales level. However, the majority of Welsh offshoots of UK-wide agencies have limited autonomy because they lack independent income raising capacity and are mostly bound by key decisions made at national level. They focus on consultation, lobbying, supplying and collecting information. However, there are two partial exceptions. The two local authority associations have achieved a substantial measure of autonomy from their national parent bodies in putting policy proposals and recommendations to the WO. Secondly, the WTUC, although financially dependent on the UK parent body, has often taken an independent line. It has consistently favoured devolution, adopted a positive attitude towards Europe, played an active part in wooing inward investment and forged close links with business interests.

In the North East, as in most English regions, institutional arrangements for economic development are complex and responsibilities fragmented. Despite the history of regional corporatism, regional economic development institutions do not command the central positions of the agencies in Scotland and Wales. Most activity, whether through Urban Development Corporations, local authorities, Training and Enterprise Councils, Enterprise Agencies or public–private partnership organisations, occurs at conurbation and local levels. Even the Northern Development Company (NDC), the region's principal economic development agency with a £6m budget, is dwarfed in resource terms by the two Urban Development Corporations and the local authorities.

Nevertheless, the most notable institutional developments over the last five years have nonetheless occurred at regional level. The Government Office for the North East (GONE) is an attempt to improve policy integration, exploit European structural funds, encourage regional partnership and advise Whitehall upon Single

Regeneration Budget (SRB) funding. It is too early to judge GONE. Sceptics claim that its autonomy will be heavily constrained by the four relevant Whitehall departments and the need to adhere to national political priorities. Far from promoting devolved, regionally-sensitive decision making, it may therefore prove a more effective way for the centre to control the region. Others are more optimistic that it will promote greater coordination in economic development and improve regional networking and strategic thinking.

A further development, partly attributable to GONE, is the establishment of the North East Chamber of Commerce (NECC), England's first regional chamber. This was created by the amalgamation of the Tyneside, Teesside and Tynedale Chambers and a simultaneous strengthening of the five local offices. NECC is intended to achieve economies of scale and critical mass, improve services to business through enhanced coordination, marketing and quality control and provide a more effective regional industrial lobby to government. Other regional institutional developments include Manufacturing Challenge, a business self-help initiative to improve manufacturing performance through emulation of best practice. The Higher Education Support for Industry Network (HESIN) is a collaborative effort by the region's Universities to apply their expertise more systematically in solving regional industry problems. The Northern Information Applications Agency promotes information technology within regional industries.

Compared with other English regions, the North East has more, comparatively influential, regional economic development institutions. NDC is the most successful of the English inward investment agencies. It results from a tripartite commitment, first agreed by the region's employers, trade unions and local authorities in the 1960s, to adopt a strategic approach to developing the region's economic infrastructure. The North of England Assembly of local authorities (NEA), which provides an united local government voice on regional issues, further typifies regional collaboration. It is widely respected and supported by its members and has taken a lead in coordinating regional economic strategy work and in establishing an office in Brussels with the support of NDC and the region's TECs.

However, the impact of North East regional institutions is limited by resource constraints and constrained autonomy. No new money is available to GONE. NDC, meanwhile, has recently experienced budget cuts in line with those of local authorities and is subject to increasingly stringent accounting mechanisms and audit controls by its government sponsors, the Department of Trade and Industry. Many other regional bodies are effectively branches of national organisations with limited discretion. For example, the NE TUC's main responsibilities are to put regional flesh on the bones of national decisions and to work in partnership with other regional interests, although Board members have influenced national headquarters. The NE CBI mainly performs a lobbying, consultative and information-gathering role and does not exercise policy making or executive powers.

Given their similar status, there are many institutional parallels between the North West and the North East. But the North West's sheer size and physical diversity and the rivalry between its two major conurbations, Merseyside and Greater Manchester, have traditionally militated against institutional mobilisation on a regional basis (Burch, 1993). It has been described as a region with many barons but no king. The fact that the airport authorities in Manchester and Liverpool have made independent expansion proposals widely regarded as being mutually exclusive is symptomatic of the internal challenges the region faces. Rather than try to break down the Manchester–Liverpool fault line when creating GORs, the government chose to develop the Merseyside Task Force into an independent GOR separate from the North West office which covers the rest of the region. Considerable care and negotiation between the GORs will be needed if the traditional divide is not to be further institutionalised.

Until recently there were just two regional economic development organisations of any note. One is INWARD, the inward investment agency created in 1986 and supported by the Invest in Britain Bureau and many, but not all, of the region's local authorities and private sector bodies. The other is NIMTECH, a technology transfer organisation. In the last five years, however, more region-wide organisations have emerged and greater interest has been shown in strategic approaches to regional economic development (Burch and Holliday, 1993; Burch and Rhodes, 1993). The region's local authorities have grouped themselves together within the North West Regional Association (NWRA). Senior business leaders have formed the North West Business Leadership Team (NWBLT). The North West Regional Partnership (NWRP) links these two, and others, together in a public–private partnership. These changes suggest a greater recognition of regional-level interdependence within the public sector and between public and private sectors. They have also been helped by the European Commission's insistence that regional economic development policies should be based on the consensual view of government, local authorities and the social partners. The UK government's partial rehabilitation of strategic planning has also encouraged the process.

NWBLT, created in 1989, is a voluntary grouping of the region's 30 major private firms which, through lobbying and promotional work, has played an important part in orchestrating regional concerns and boosting private sector involvement. NWBLT enables the private sector to play a wider strategic role, encouraged by the European Commission which argued that the region needed to have a clearer economic development strategy in order to maximise EU support and resources after the review of Objective 2 assistance in 1993. This prompted NWBLT and NWRA to jointly commission a major study which analysed the North West economy and proposed an economic development strategy for the region. One of its key recommendations was the creation of NWRP which would draw members from the two organisations plus other regional agencies in the region such as universities, TECs and trades unions.

NWRP was duly created in 1994, charged with promoting the economic and social well-being of the region, coordinating partners' inputs to further strategy development and implementation, presenting its case to government and the European Union, promoting a clear identity and positive image and extending links with Europe. But the NWRP is only a promotional and coordinating body and lacks the executive powers of the regional bodies in Scotland and Wales or even NDC in the North East. It is a fragile regeneration vehicle and its ability to implement the regional strategy largely depends upon the goodwill, influence and resources of its partners.

Chapter 4

Institutions, strategies and regional economic competitiveness

Strategic responses to regional economic problems

It is frequently argued that an essential prerequisite to policy success is the establishment of clear mechanisms through which regional problems can be identified and tackled; that is, a means of deriving a development agenda and delivering an economic strategy. Equally importantly, that strategy must be communicated widely, implemented effectively and make some impact upon the economic competitiveness of the region. This chapter assesses these arguments. Two elements – strategy and implementation – are first addressed. The second section examines perceptions about the impact of regional institutions.

The formation of regional economic strategies

Each of the case study regions has an economic development strategy. But they differ in their origins, natures and degrees of formality. Scotland has the most coherent and broadly supported strategic framework and the best-resourced institutions to deliver programmes. The strength and coverage of the LECs in pursuing local economic development and labour market programmes makes them the most powerful set of local institutions in the four regions. They fit into a Scotland-wide framework through a chain of accountability that runs upward, first to their parent bodies (SE and HIE) and then onto the SOEID and, ultimately, the Scottish Secretary of State. This relatively new system has occasioned some confusion (Scottish Select Committee, 1994). The consensus, however, is that relations between SOEID and SE/HIE, and between the agencies and the LECs, are slowly being clarified as each link in the chain comes to understand the limits of its autonomy more clearly.

Scottish Enterprise is the critical link in the chain. Its capacity and role means it provides strategic direction in negotiation with the LECs, the SOEID and other leading agencies. It does so in a formal sense through strategy reviews which in theory are internal but in practice are widely and informally consulted upon. The most recent, major review identified key sectoral clusters on which Scotland's competitive strengths depend and charted a strategy by which Scotland's economic agencies could effect change. SE's strategy drew upon widespread consensus that 'manufacturing matters' (CBI Scottish Manufacturing Group, 1994). The analysis accepted that services remain the best hope for future job generation in Scotland's comparatively service-dominated economy (Figure 5). But it recognised that a large proportion of services, including many fast growing and locally rooted ones, are not independent but are consumed as inputs to manufacturing.

It also recognised that the long-running and successful practice of luring foreign, particularly American, companies to Scotland through public subsidy and low unit labour costs would need to change (STUC, 1992; SCDI, 1993). This was partly a reaction to the changing policy environment; the combined package of assistance once available from the old SDA, UK regional policy grants, Scotland's former New Town corporations and LiS had become less potent as a result of national policy change. But there was also growing concern that incoming plants often perform relatively low-grade tasks and generate limited spin-offs for indigenous suppliers (McCalman, 1992; Turok, 1993). Furthermore, growing global competition from low wage economies meant Scotland's future competitiveness had to be based upon the quality of its products rather than their ability to compete on price. A strategy of adding value, although it might create fewer jobs in the short term, would help develop competitive potential and hence retain and create more secure employment in the longer term.

These concerns led to a rationalisation of SE's priorities and a greater commitment to creating and sustaining Scottish-owned companies and helping them compete. A variety of measures to achieve this have been proposed (Scottish Enterprise, 1995):

- boosting the rate of new firm formation by promoting the culture and practice of entrepreneurship;

- trying to change personal and institutional attitudes to risk;

- smoothing company access to finance and support;

- reducing the out-migration of Scottish talent;

- raising the level of product and process innovation by encouraging company research and development and business–university links;

- promoting the benefits of training and development to companies;

- strengthening the linkages between foreign-owned companies and local suppliers;

- lobbying for improved road, rail and airport infrastructures.

Scottish Enterprise's concerns are widely shared within the Scottish policy community. Internally, disagreements tend to centre on sectoral priorities. Whilst some stress diversification and new sectoral development, others argue for the selective modernisation of older sectors. Such sectors, including textiles and mechanical engineering, are acknowledged as being in overall decline but it is argued that they contain a core of vigorous and competitive firms who could protect Scotland's competitive base if given help in the diversification of markets.

Strategic agencies in Wales operate within a less specific policy framework. The WDA cited the Secretary of State's strategic guidance and internal reviews, or more recently the published Corporate Plan, when describing its overall approach. The DBRW, in contrast, has prepared more formal strategy statements. Recently, the joint chairmanship of WDA and DBRW has resulted in closer policy coordination between the two agencies. There is less connection with external bodies on strategy formation than in Scotland. The Council for Welsh Districts has prepared economic strategy statements for Wales in the past. Similarly, the Institute for Welsh Affairs provided a vision of Wales' economic future and a statement of strategic intent in its *Wales 2010* document. Such attempts have not, however, generated much dialogue on strategic development issues in governmental circles.

This might stem from fears that all-embracing strategies might become a political platform. Or it might simply demonstrate the power and independence of the WDA. But it also reflects the absence of a strong, parochial Welsh establishment. Compared to Scotland, the indigenous policy making and corporate elite in Wales is relatively weak. As a partial consequence, conflicts at the sub-Wales level are both sharper and more difficult to resolve. The Welsh equivalent of the 'Scottish card', which can be played whenever there is a need to unite and discipline interest groups in support of a 'national' cause, is weaker and more difficult to invoke. As a result, Welsh Secretaries of State have not been quite as susceptible to national 'establishment' pressures as their Scottish equivalents.

With the recent subdivision of WDA into three sub-regional offices, the agency is attempting to take sub-Wales economic differences into account by preparing integrated development strategies for the sub-regions. Despite the largely implicit nature of the strategic policy framework, there has been a fair degree of consensus on the priority WDA and DBRW have attached to inward investment, land reclamation and property development. Local authorities have broadly supported these aims whilst at the same time quibbling over locational issues, style of delivery and some policy areas such as town centre regeneration which they argue could successfully be pursued locally. Although in one sense the effectiveness of the WDA and DBRW has obviated the need for an all-encompassing strategy, a sense of teamwork and inclusion and clarity over respective roles might have been greater within a clearer strategic framework.

In both the North East and the North West, the EC's insistence that an agreed regional strategy was needed to secure structural funds prompted strategy formulation. In the North East, the NEA coordinated strategy preparation with the support of government departments, local authorities, regional offices of quangos, the utilities, educational and training institutions, transport operators and private sector representatives. The strategy incorporates eight objectives covering the following areas:

- business support, development and application of new technology and research and development;

- investment in human resources;

- improvement of physical infrastructure;

- development of transport and communications;

- enhancement of natural environment and image;

- promotion of tourism;

- targeted support for severely disadvantaged areas.

The regional development strategy spawned further strategic thinking. Higher education institutions in the North East, for example, took the lead in putting together a Regional Innovation and Technology Strategy. This attempts to address the low incidence of business starts in technologically advanced areas, firms' lack of involvement in research and development and the absence of government research establishments by improving research and development structures and technology support to meet identified customer needs. Although progress in the North West has been more difficult, there is nonetheless a high degree of support for the main elements of the regional strategy prepared for NWRA and NWBLT (Pieda, 1993). These include fostering the region's production and export capacities through exploiting the knowledge base; skills enhancement and business support measures to improve the region's physical environment and image; and developing internal and external transport links.

Strategy implementation

Regional institutions do not act merely as ringmasters in regional strategy preparation. Their status, powers, level of autonomy and relationships with other strategic bodies have an important bearing upon the likelihood of successful implementation. Experience in the North West shows that whilst consensus has been reached on the broad content of the strategy, the lack of a regional executive agency and the dependence of the North West Partnership upon its local and sub-regional members for support on particular initiatives has impeded progress. The NWP is attempting to flesh out the strategy in greater detail by creating a network of working parties, each concentrating upon key themes within the regional strategy. Their current priorities include: transport links, a human resources development strategy, a technology and innovation programme, a regional information society project, a seed capital fund and a strategy to create a portfolio of strategic sites.

But it is difficult to secure voluntary backing for regional initiatives when there is only a muted sense of regional identity and when local funds are stretched. Where regional executive structures do not exist, a strong sense of regional consciousness is even more essential to the prospects of success. The negative experience of INWARD in the North West is instructive here. INWARD has a low level of funding, based on voluntary contributions. It has experienced difficulty in generating a track record to provide legitimacy and has struggled to prevent sub-regional marketing initiatives contradicting, rather than complementing, regional promotional activity. These factors have undermined its performance in comparison with its competitors in the other regions.

Even in Wales and Scotland, where similar executive structures are better developed and resourced, variable levels of consensus and legitimacy are important influences on performance. The depth and frequency of informal interaction between Ministers and senior officials in the SO and leading decision makers in other Scottish public agencies and the corporate sector engenders more consensus than is the case in Wales. To its supporters, the Scottish corporatist tradition ensures that Scotland's public executive agencies are held accountable to Scottish opinion in a highly informal way which nonetheless ensures that UK policy developments are sensitised to Scottish circumstances (Moore and Booth, 1989). To its detractors, Scottish corporatism is a system whereby a largely unelected elite which is comfortable with – indeed part of – the status quo makes decisions and strikes bargains behind closed doors. Whichever view one holds, elite consensus undoubtedly helps imbue SE and other economic agencies with legitimacy and clout beyond their formal competences and ensures a high level of moral and practical support for their work.

In Wales, solidarity between decision-making elites and the regional development agencies is more precarious. Although WDA and DBRW are widely admired in a technical sense, recent scandals concerning them have caused political storms which, at least temporarily, have badly damaged their reputations and affected their performance. The Welsh Labour Party used the agency's malpractice, symbolically, to discredit quangocracy and highlight the democratic deficit. The government, meanwhile, distanced itself by tightening controls and replacing senior agency personnel. Concern about malpractice amongst LECs in Scotland, by contrast, produced a media flurry, a Scottish Select Committee enquiry and a sober debate about reform which has not seriously threatened the performance or legitimacy of the system. This suggests that regional structures matter but culture and politics are equally important. NDC's remarkable achievements in view of its modest budget mimics sophisticated SO and WO practice by, for example, developing supplier associations to embed inward investment into the regional economy. Regional collaboration, political consensus and effective interorganisational networking can clearly achieve a great deal, even in the absence of strong executive structures.

There was a widespread feeling within the case study regions that certain economic development functions require a regional approach, backed by regional institutional capacity. This was felt to apply most to inward investment, strategic networking, the deployment of specialist expertise and the raising of international awareness. The theme of inward investment provides a good comparison of the regions. Here, the lead given by LiS, WDA, NDC and INWARD, despite big variations in their performance and perceived effectiveness, is crucial to whatever success regions had had in attracting inward investment. This reflected their abilities to put together an adequately resourced, well-structured and coordinated package to woo investors, to encourage other partners to make and deliver promises, to provide a continuous point of contact, including aftercare, to project a consistent image of the region and to have sufficient resources to maintain overseas offices in key markets.

Inward investment agencies are also well placed to encourage the reorientation of local supplier firms towards incoming firms. This is crucial since organic ties between regional firms encourage reinvestment by incoming firms and the possible development of higher order functions such as research and development, thus maximising local spin-offs. Performance here was again seen as variable, with WDA and NDC viewed as increasingly effective and INWARD, along with LiS and the LECs, as less so. To some extent, this reflected the varying size of the gap, in technology and sophistication, between incoming firms and local suppliers. Where this gap is larger, as it has been with some incomers to Scotland, the task of local agencies in encouraging supplier linkages is made more difficult. However, the effort put into this task was smaller, and less coordinated, in Scotland and the North West. The WDA, by contrast, is seen as a pioneer in developing regional supply chains in strategically important sectors like automotive, aerospace and medical functions and in systematically attempting to attract inward investment to fill gaps in capacity.

There was a general feeling that sub-regional attempts to 'go it alone' in luring inward investment posed the danger of duplication, contradictory messages, and a parochiality which could potentially undermine the credibility of those involved and deter investors. In the English regions, the territorial agencies in Scotland and Wales were perceived as having a clear competitive edge over the NDC and INWARD. Better funding was one reason for this. Another was their ability to integrate promotional/development and educational programmes with strategic sites and premises programmes. Their capacity to use the good offices of their respective Secretaries of State, assuming they were prepared to debate and perhaps 'go to war' with Cabinet colleagues over a particular issue, is also important. Separate departmental funding by government of inward investment programmes, technology transfer and export missions was thought to hinder the effectiveness of the English agencies.

Case study evidence also suggests that another advantage of regional agencies is their ability to exploit economies of scale. This enables the employment of specialist expertise which helps solve complex local problems and resolve strategic issues in a non-political, technical fashion. The Land Authority for Wales, for example, applies specialist legal and land management skills to multi-dimensional problems such as the assembly of town centre sites with diverse ownership in a way which would be beyond the capacity of local agencies. LAW has also provided valuable impartial advice on disputed matters such as the prospects for attracting development to sites in local authority land banks.

The strategic remit of the WO, SO, SE, WDA and DBRW has also enabled them to target assistance at key economic sectors and strategic skill shortages. DBRW, for example, has successfully revived the rural food sector by developing and marketing Welsh cheeses and lamb. WDA's use of specialist knowledge of the automotive sector and, to a more limited extent, of the aerospace and pharmaceutical industries, together with modern industrial practices, has encouraged the formation of the largest concentration of supplier associations in Europe. And the WO has targeted new apprenticeships scheme monies entirely at remedying the shortage of intermediate technicians. Local and regional organisations in the English regions have generally found it much more difficult to tackle regional problems with such strategic purpose.

The ability of regional agencies to act in an intermediary and catalytic role clearly promotes denser patterns of regional networking. The SO and WO's control of all the relevant economic development functions has reduced the time and effort involved in putting together multi-disciplinary programmes, reconciling departmental priorities and orchestrating different regional organisations. Response rates, for example to major industrial closures, are invariably quicker and more effective. The concentration of political power and key personnel in other strategic organisations within Cardiff and Edinburgh's policy-making centres has also facilitated networking. Novel initiatives such as the Welsh Medical Technology Forum, which involves the sharing of technology and marketing resources between manufacturers, suppliers, the NHS and educational establishments, would not have happened but for WO coordination. Similarly, the WO's wide remit enables it to orchestrate action by consulting widely and then communicating clearly to different organisations where they should focus their energies to meet overall targets.

This is happening in the education, training and enterprise sphere following the publication of an Action Agenda entitled *People and Prosperity*. The WDA has also played a leading role in the production of a Welsh Technology Plan. This seeks to develop the interface between academic institutions and 'leading-edge' small and medium-sized enterprises throughout Wales. The related virtual technopole project which is building a network of advanced business service providers which uses the Internet to compensate for poor transport connections. Other strategic partnerships and networks kick-started by the WO, DBRW and WDA include the Mid-Wales Export Association, the Mid-Wales Manufacturing Group, Urban Joint Ventures and West Wales Task Force.

In Scotland, many of the main economic development partnerships develop at the local level, with LECs rather than SE as the prime movers. But added value is gained from networking at the Scottish level, too. A SE scheme for capping business loans and guaranteeing a stable financial environment for firms offers a good illustration. Here, SE and the major Scottish-owned banks were able to agree on a scheme whereby banks provided loans to firms and SE agreed to absorb any increase in repayments that might result from interest rate fluctuations above a pre-agreed limit. The scheme aroused Treasury suspicion but SE, backed by the SO and helped by Cabinet-level intervention from the Secretary of State, successfully argued that the scheme represented a Scottish answer to a Scottish problem. There was no necessary implication for the rest of the UK; but if the scheme worked well it could be tried elsewhere. This example shows how strong public–private sector relationships, corporate self-interest, common 'regionalist' politics, institutional clout and good political connections can generate initiatives which would be virtually impossible to replicate within the English regions.

The evidence of this project suggests that regional capacity is important in raising international awareness. Success within the global economy requires increasingly high and sophisticated levels of internationalisation. Governmental bodies need to adopt outward-looking attitudes to influence global politics and EU policies and funding priorities. Private companies need to be aware of new market opportunities, potential strategic partners and world class standards of best practice. Agencies and businesses in both public and private sectors need to be prepared to forge international strategic alliances and commercial links. In the case study examples, the WO has helped cement inter-regional political and economic alliances such as the Four Motors, involving governments, development agencies and businesses from Baden-Wurttemberg, Catalonia, Rhones Alpes and Lombardy. The more entrepreneurial WDA has translated such political agreements into commercial reality by acting as a marriage bureau, bringing together 112 joint private sector projects in Germany, Italy, Spain and France over the last five years.

International awareness is also needed with regard to EU funds. Here, regional institutions have played an important coordinating role in generating strategies to guide fund allocation. WO, NEA and NWP each orchestrated regional development strategies which guide the use of Objective 2 funds. SE and WDA partially sponsor Scotland Europa and the Wales European Centre respectively. These organisations raise awareness of EU funding opportunities, give early warning of legislative changes, supply information on programme regulations and provide a vehicle for lobbying and becoming known and respected by Directorates General. Although NEA and its partners have set up a similar organisation for the North East, it is less well staffed and resourced. The North East regional institutional framework is viewed positively by the EU in terms of policy innovation, especially on telecommunications issues. But there is little sign as yet that the region has developed a coherent 'foreign policy'.

As with many other English regions, 'grantsmanship' appears more important to the North East than the European policy debates and networking initiatives which typify Welsh and Scottish presence in Brussels. The North West does not retain a Brussels representative. However, Merseyside partners have just opened an office and a Manchester representative operates from the Brussels office of Lancashire Enterprise Limited, a sub-regional enterprise agency. The growing knowledge of regional agencies about EU matters and their proficiency in tapping structural funds has opened up additional commercial opportunities and raised the international profiles of Wales and Scotland in particular to an extent which would not otherwise have been possible.

The level of specialist expertise within SE, HIE, WDA and DBRW has also meant that EU programmes in technology transfer and specialist business services, such as STRIDE and SPRINT, have been better utilised in boosting the level of regional innovation. SE/LiS and WDA's international activities and supplier development work have also played a part in increasing awareness of international standards of best practice in manufacturing. In the North East and North West, there is mounting evidence that the region's higher educational institutions and the GORs are beginning to realise that such funds can be used to foster research and development and technology transfer to promote regional development. In the past, a lack of regional institutional capacity and coordinating mechanisms has meant that progress in the English regions has lagged in this respect. However, this is less the case in the North East than in the North West.

Regional institutional capacity: gaps and limitations

Gauging the relationship between regional institutional capacity and regional economic performance is primarily a matter of judgement. The overall message from our research was that the influence of regional institutions on processes of economic innovation and change is limited but far from negligible. It is limited because regional institutional machinery has purchase over relatively few of the resources needed to effect economic change. It would be unrealistic, therefore, to expect the various institutional frameworks in the four regions to have engineered miraculous turnarounds. In all four cases economic circumstances are less promising than those faced by 'luckier' regions closer to the centre of European economic gravity.

But there was clear consensus that the institutional machinery in Scotland and Wales was better able to understand, articulate, engage with and act upon regional problems than were their counterparts in England. To some extent this reflects variations in levels of resource. Scottish Enterprise, for example, is grant aided by government to the tune of £380m per year. NDC, although with fewer responsibilities, struggles along with around £6m worth of support from the Department of Trade and Industry, local authorities and Directorates General of the European Commission. Since finances buy knowledge, expertise, influence and supporters, commentators in the English regions are clearly right to argue that they are at a substantial disadvantage compared to Scotland and Wales. The other key point to emerge, however, is that institutions, whatever their formal powers, work better when their *raisons d'être* and priorities are seen as legitimate within civil society – that is, when they are part of a wider social consensus. Thus the sum of the institutional parts in Scotland compared to Wales, and the North East compared to the North West, was seen as greater not because the parts were very different but because intangible factors such as legitimacy, consensus and inter-agency networking meant they combined more effectively.

Beyond such broad judgements, it is difficult to specify precisely what variations in institutional capacity mean in terms of economic change. Inherent difficulties in understanding causes and effects are magnified by the fact that neither are easily addressed via standard statistics. It is extremely difficult, for example, to discount other variables, for example factor availability and cost, quality of infrastructure and central government/EU grant incentives and to account for economic geography considerations such as market access. It is also difficult to address the additionality problem: how well local and national economies would have performed in the absence of regional institutions. To even begin to make sense of such variables would demand enormous forward strides in concepts, methods and empirical research. Such advances would be very welcome but their results would still most likely be hotly disputed.

This study was not a technical exercise aimed at overcoming such difficulties. Rather, it attempted to infer relationships from available 'hard' data and perceptions. The field of inward investment offers a good example of how much can and can not reasonably be inferred from the evidence available. Gross figures are probably easiest to come by and there is relatively clear evidence that regional development agencies have had an impact. It is still difficult, though, to assess the importance of institutional factors accurately, not least because of the shortage of data on jobs and investment associated with inward investment projects. Nevertheless, there was a broad correlation between the level of perceived institutional effectiveness about inward investment in the four regions and the available statistical evidence.

Hill and Munday (1991) argue that lower wage costs and financial assistance accounted for almost 80% of the variation in inward capital investment in Wales relative to other regions in the period 1979-89. However, since 1992 Wales' relative performance in securing new inward investment projects and creating and saving jobs has declined sharply and now compares unfavourably with Scotland, the North West and the North East (see Figure 4). While the slowdown in volumes of inward investment following the completion of the Single Market and loss of Assisted Area and Objective 2 status in parts of Wales may be partly to blame, Wales' poor performance in relation to similar regions suggests that institutional factors – the tarnished image of the WDA, poor staff morale, the hiatus caused by extensive internal restructuring – has played an important part.

Institutional factors, in other words, can result in regions over- or under-achieving upon whatever potential their structural advantages or disadvantages bequeath them. The last couple of years apart, WDA, DBRW and their partners must receive substantial credit for the improved performance of the Welsh economy relative to the UK norm. Given the weakness of indigenous industry, the consistency and scale of inward investment has been crucial to the reversal of Welsh fortunes in terms of employment, unemployment, manufacturing output and GDP. Between 1979 and 1991, Wales attracted over 14% of UK total of inward investment, despite having only 4.4% of total UK employment. Foreign inward investment now accounts for about a third of total manufacturing employment. Many incoming companies adopt advanced quality management systems and manufacturing techniques which have boosted output and GDP. In mid-Wales alone, unemployment rates at the time DBRW was designated were 50% above the UK average, whereas they are now 20% below. There appears to be a close relationship between the number of jobs created by DBRW and overall growth in jobs in the sub-regional economy.

The impact of the inward investment work led in Scotland by LiS – by common consent, the one UK agency in this field whose competitors are international rather than domestic – has been even more impressive. During the 1980s, output in the electronics sector, largely based upon inward investment by foreign firms from the US and more recently from the Pacific Rim, rose by 275%. Computers now account for 30% of the export values of Scottish goods. In comparison with Wales and Scotland, NDC has a comparatively modest budget. But in absolute terms, over a sustained period, the region has managed to secure an above average proportion of jobs per head of population relative to the UK average and other comparable regions such as the North West (Figure 4). Invest in Britain Bureau statistics suggest the superior performance of the North East cannot be put down simply to the scale of incentives for manufacturing investment since the region performed comparatively well in both non-manufacturing and manufacturing investment projects.

Support for NDC by the North East's local authorities is crucial. It is reflected in NDC's per capita income. NDC's 56.2p compared very favourably with INWARD's 16.7p and the national average for regional development organisations of 22.2p. It also reflects the fact that 80% of local authorities think NDC promotes the region effectively overseas (Peck and Tickell, 1992). Key foreign investors like Samsung and Nissan have indicated that favourable experiences of operating in the region, and the support received from NDC and its partners, have spurred them to invest further in the region. Conversely, the North West has long achieved only about half the new overseas inward investment projects that would be expected given its population. Such differences in part reflect agency performance and calibre. But the ability of the North East's economic development bodies to act as a team has undoubtedly strengthened NDC's hand.

On the more general question of whether there is a regional institutional deficit in the UK which prevents regions from attaining their full economic potential, the research found very different views. For the non-English nations, which have stronger 'regional' institutional capacity, the critical question is whether more powers and responsibilities should be wrested from Whitehall and Westminster or whether Scotland and Wales should have their own, fully independent, Parliaments and executives. In the English regions, the limits of ambition do not generally rise beyond achieving the degree of devolution and executive capacity that Scotland and Wales already possess.

There is a clear perception within the North East that gaps exist in regional institutional capacity with regard to innovation and technology transfer, regional banking and venture capital, research and development and image promotion. The strengthening of regional institutions such as NDC, it is generally felt, would help. However, views differ on whether larger changes in regional institutional arrangements would improve economic performance. A majority of interviewees believed they would. They argued that the powers of existing regional institutions should be consolidated and extended, possibly by granting tourism and property development responsibilities. They also argued that they should be made accountable to an elected regional assembly. The economic benefits of this, it was felt, would include:

- greater regional policy innovation and joint working;
- policies more attuned to regional circumstances and indigenous productive potential;
- more long-term strategies and policy continuity;
- a stronger regional voice in Europe;
- a greater sense of ownership of strategic projects.

Other interviewees remained unconvinced. Some felt GONE should be given time to demonstrate its potential as an orchestrator, networker and broker and that new regional economic development powers, responsibilities and structures could introduce unnecessary rigidity. While recognising the need for more regional strategic thinking, this group was not convinced that an elected regional assembly would necessarily perform such a role or improve regional prospects. They feared decisions would be taken on local political, rather than strategic economic, grounds. They also doubted the calibre and capacity of local politicians and felt change risked creating additional bureaucracy. A small minority suggested that a revival of local government and enhanced resources for local economic development, coupled with the rehabilitation of regional policy and greater sensitivity to regional needs by central government, would preclude the need for further institutional capacity at the regional level.

In the North West there was a widely held view that the region would perform better if there was more regional collaboration and if the shortage of regional venture capital funds, higher education–business links and specialised business support structures could be addressed. It was readily agreed that regional action must extend beyond inward investment. But there were differing views about whether a traditional failure to do so necessarily reflected a regional institutional deficit. Support for a regional development agency along Welsh lines was somewhat muted and many commentators argued that the North West's problems were as much cultural as institutional. Hence the region is seen as lagging behind not merely Scotland and Wales, which are different institutionally, but also the North East, which is not. The history of economic diversity and political rivalries have, at least until recently, prevented the emergence of regional networks and a regional consciousness. That in turn has precluded the emergence of regional institutions with authority and legitimacy.

The most widely shared view of business leaders, senior academics and local authority figures is that any enhancement of regional institutional capacity should proceed on a voluntary basis. More formal institutional changes, many claim, could divert attention from essential coalition building and strategy implementation activities. The disruptions caused by recent local government reforms have accentuated such worries. It was argued that networks, people and measures to improve the performance of current institutions should be the targets for change. These depend, in turn, upon shifts in attitudes and practices to encourage greater openness, trust and transparency in regional resource allocation. 'Process, not structure' is seen as the point of entry for improved regional performance. There is little enthusiasm for embarking on another round of costly, time-consuming and disruptive reform designed to address the fragmentation caused by a proliferation of economic development agencies at sub-regional level. More hopes are pinned upon developing networks between the institutions.

In Scotland the real bone of contention is who is in charge of the institutional machinery, not the nature of the machinery itself. This expresses itself in two ways. A less explosive debate concerns the accountability of Scotland's economic development bodies to local and national (Scottish) opinion. This emerges, for example, in worries expressed by STUC and CoSLA about the extent to which LECs work alongside local authorities in developing economic agenda and programmes for their areas. Both would prefer local authorities to have a greater say in local economic development decision making. But, pragmatically, they do not campaign against LECs – nor bodies like SE, LiS and STI – per se. The deeper rooted, more sensitive debate is whether Scotland's institutional machinery can serve Scottish interests adequately under current political and administrative arrangements. For a majority of Scots, the answer is clearly 'no', since opinion polls regularly show a majority in favour of devolution and a significant minority in favour of independence. At heart, then, this is a debate about democracy within the UK and who controls the 'national' destiny. It is not about the institutional tools available to try to shape that destiny. As such, it is not central to this report. And yet it is also a debate about regional economic development. It appears to be assumed by all proponents of change that improvements in economic performance would automatically follow. Only change the rider, it seems, and the horse will run better.

At its most basic, this argument seems to reflect reasonably widespread confidence that 'a nation at peace with itself' will simply do better in all respects. Once one looks for substantive evidence, however, this is a very complex argument to sustain (Lee, 1995). It depends upon a range of economic and political assumptions, for example about levels of taxation and future patterns of UK public expenditure, whose character would to some extent be determined by the nature of the change itself and in other respects cannot be anticipated. Of the major voices in the debate, only the Scottish National Party have given any firm indication of the sorts of mechanisms through which economic performance is expected to be improved (SNP, 1992b). Even then, reform of economic development machinery plays a negligible role compared to a radically different approach to taxation and expenditure. The absence of debate on institutions appears to reflect widespread agreement that Scottish institutions in general, and those in the economic development field which arouse envy within English regions in particular, serve Scotland well enough not to need to undergo major reform.

Most of the comments about Scotland also apply to Wales. Currently there is little complaint about regional institutions in terms of their resources, powers and effectiveness. It is their perceived lack of accountability and an alleged high-handed and non-inclusive style which has occasioned most criticism and led to calls for WDA and DBRW to act more in consort with local partners and for the WO to enhance its coordinating role and give a stronger strategic lead. If anything, there is more pressure in Wales for power to be passed from the regional to the local level as new unitary local authorities sense the opportunity for local government to regain status by requesting central government to grant the necessary resources and powers. The WO's direct involvement in Welsh local government reform and their interest in seeing it succeed has strengthened their bargaining position. A parallel debate in Scotland has sprung from a very different source. There, the current Secretary of State is arguing that the true meaning of subsidiarity in Scotland should entail the devolution of powers from the Scottish Office to local authorities, not from London to Edinburgh.

Protagonists claim that the creation of a Welsh Assembly would lead to a sense of shared purpose and self-confidence, legitimacy for regional institutions, policies suited to Welsh needs, integrated approaches to regional, technology and training policies, a good deal from Europe and a spur to self-help. However, the present system already displays many of these qualities due to joint working at the all-Wales level and the increased interorganisational networking attributable to the WO, the WDA and others. Opinions differ as to whether Wales could secure more resources from Europe with an Assembly. Some suspect the government continues to use EU funding to offset national expenditures. With the EU tightening up on additionality, though, it is not clear why an Assembly would improve upon present arrangements.

As in Scotland, it is not clear that the creation of a Welsh Assembly would necessarily enhance economic performance. Certainly, business leaders do not have much confidence that this would be the case. A recent survey in Wales showed ambivalence. Some respondents believed an Assembly could have positive effects on the image of Wales in Europe. Others feared additional bureaucracy and costs. Most wanted further clarification of powers, financing and membership before committing themselves. In Scotland, business feeling remains firmly anti-independence. But it becomes less anti-devolution as the possibility of a Labour government grows. The key issue for Scottish businesses has been the potential costs of change. Since Labour has promised to limit the additional taxation powers of a Scottish Parliament to varying income tax within a narrow band around the UK level, there are few fears now about direct business costs. On indirect costs, the much-exaggerated fear is that market disadvantage could arise because foreign trading partners and customers would perceive change, whatever its reality, as denoting political uncertainty and upheaval.

Business leaders in Wales and Scotland were by no means alone in suspecting that a more democratic but 'thicker' system of decision making, unless it were somehow channelled into serious examination of economic issues, could simply politicise and embed problems rather than provide the means to resolve them. On this view, a Parliament or an Assembly could become an arena in which parish pump politics, parochial tendencies, sub-national tensions and disputes over the division of functions between local government and regional quangos could become magnified. As one interviewee remarked, the Whitehall model means "priority has to be given to the urgent rather than the important...It would be easy to fill the whole day drafting answers to Parliamentary questions which enable the Minister to say nothing, cleverly". Measured against such a scenario, some argue that current executive capacity in Wales and Scotland is relatively lean, politically unconstrained and proactive. Attempts to justify change on the grounds that improved economic performance would follow therefore seem to contain a leap of faith which many of the intended beneficiaries are reluctant to make.

Chapter 5

Regionalisation: the two key questions revisited

Regionalisation and regional government

Chapter 1 identified two important themes in the current debate about regionalisation which were examined in the research. These can be reduced to two propositions. Both are used to support arguments for constitutional change and regional government. The first is that recent regionalisation trends have so strengthened non-elected regional governing capacity that regional government, in England just as in the UK's small stateless nations, could be achieved by simply democratising what already exists. The second is that the link between elected regional institutional capacity and regional economic performance supports an economic case for regional government. On the evidence of this study, neither proposition is wholly convincing. That does not mean there is no demand for greater regional autonomy, for regional government in England and for further devolution or independence in Scotland and Wales. Nor does it mean that regional government structures, or other forms of regional administration, cannot make a positive contribution to regional economic health. But it does mean that the arguments for change have not become appreciably stronger, or weaker, as a result of recent trends.

Chapter 2 described the different, often contradictory, impulses that lie behind the recent growth in regional executive capacity and activity and the forms it has taken. It suggested the net result is a mass of barely-related initiatives, operating within a variety of inconsistent boundaries. This fragmented 'system' primarily serves the government's convenience in streamlining administration, cutting costs, developing 'government by contract', pushing the process of priority setting further down the governmental system, regulating regional utility markets and retaining control over the direction, but not the minutiae, of policy. The exceptions found by the project's audit were either voluntaristic, bottom-up initiatives by local authorities, designed to overcome fragmentation and duplication or, in a small number of cases, organisations which illustrated some recognition by government of the need to encourage regional partnerships.

Regional *autonomy to* achieve a variety of goals has been marginally extended in a patchy, ad hoc way and selective decision-making capacity at regional level has grown. But regional *autonomy from* other levels of government has not been enhanced. Indeed, insofar as new regional bodies have taken functions from local authorities, the process has produced centralisation. The autonomy of regional organisations is strictly limited. In most cases central government determines the policy framework, sets performance targets, appoints key personnel and provides most of the financial resources. In others, the youth and voluntaristic nature of regional agencies and groupings often means that they have not built up the regional profile, trust, credibility and legitimacy which might carry them onto the next, more secure and robust, stage of evolution. The chaotic regionalisation of the last fifteen years has not produced a network of institutions which could easily or quickly be merged, granted legal or constitutional status and tax-raising powers or made geographically coherent and subjected to popular election. Any move to regional government structures in England, therefore, would have to start with a blueprint that was radically different from the current situation. Effectively, it would need to start from scratch.

The case for regional *government*, as opposed to other sorts of regional institution, therefore remains unchanged. Despite the claims about efficiency and effectiveness advanced by the various camps in the debate, adjudication between them is not a technical matter. At heart, it is a political decision about where democracy properly lies; about who should have a say in what sort of decisions. It is about inputs, rather than outputs; processes rather than results. However, it has become confused with arguments about results, too. Amongst the proponents of further democratisation are groups who claim, against each other's logic, that a system of regional government will help each region attain its full economic potential whilst also providing the means for reducing disparities between regions. It is to the economic effects of enhanced regional autonomy that the report now turns.

Regional institutions and economic competitiveness

Chapter 4 demonstrated that most proponents of devolution and regional democratisation assume that positive economic changes would inevitably follow. A Scottish Parliament, a Welsh Assembly or a regional authority in England is 'sold', at least in part, with an implicit promise that it would improve the prosperity of the peoples and businesses within its territory. This idea is often backed by claims that evidence for such a link is readily found elsewhere in Europe. It is argued that regions covered by highly autonomous, constitutionally grounded, well resourced and democratically elected tiers of government are the high economic achievers in Europe and will attain greater relative prosperity in the future. Regions that lack such characteristics, or are not given them by the enlightened decentralisation policies of national governments, will fall further behind. Thus:

> [o]rganisational capacity, in terms of political and economic institutions, will be a key determiner of economic success. It is crucial to have the right institutions at regional level, so that they can bring together all the key participants in each region's economy. (Labour Party, 1995: 11)

There are four problems with such arguments. None of them entirely negate the overall case they are said to support but they do deserve further analysis. First, they polarise debate by suggesting there is a growing gulf between the UK and other EU countries in terms of sub-national institutional structures and decentralist trends. Second, they overestimate both the level of autonomy that even the best-endowed regional tiers of government have and the impact they have upon economic development. Third, they falsely ascribe a number of characteristics which facilitate economic competitiveness in regions covered by elected governments to the institutional machinery controlled by such governments. Fourth, they pay too much attention to *autonomy from* and too little to *autonomy to*. That is, they underestimate the contribution to successful regional strategy building and project development played by non-governmental, even non-institutional, forces as opposed to regional governments.

The UK out of step in Europe?

On the first two points, it is clear that there is enormous heterogeneity in sub-national governmental structures across Europe. Indeed, there are almost as many arrangements for the intermediate tiers of government between national and local/municipal levels – departments, regions, counties, autonomous communities, Länder, provinces – as there are countries (Sharpe, 1993). As the European Commission found when devising its NUTS classification system for sub-national data collection, these intermediate units vary substantially in size and status. The populations of some European 'regions', for example, are smaller than those of certain UK cities. And 'regional' institutions vary widely in their relative autonomy from other levels of government and in the extent to which the areas they cover make economic sense (Rhodes, 1995a).

The idea that regional 'units' have an economic rationale, which corresponds to travel-to-work areas and takes in the economic gravity field around major centres of population, is well established in technocratic regional planning literature. But it is rarely borne out in reality. Thus even in Germany, whose Federal system is often argued to be the most rational and decentralised in Europe, there are anomalies. For example, suburbs and areas of concentrated economic activity that depend upon Hamburg and Bremen fall outside the constrained borders of their respective city states and within one or more other Länder. The difficulties for 'regional' economic policy making caused by fragmented administration is just as acute in these two cases as it is elsewhere.

Care also needs to be taken in analysing the importance of decentralisation in different countries. Decentralist trends say nothing about the absolute extent of decentralisation in that 'decentralising' does not necessarily mean 'decentralised' (Bennett, 1990). So, for example, a centralising Denmark remains much less centralised, in absolute terms, than a decentralising France. The notion that a compulsion to decentralise has recently swept across continental Europe is also a little misleading. Some countries have taken a road similar to the UK one. In Denmark, for example, the only 'regional' authority – for Greater Copenhagen – was abolished in the 1980s. Since then, functions have selectively been withdrawn from some of Denmark's counties. Central government has created and encouraged specific, non-elected agencies for economic development. Elsewhere, new subnational units or tiers of government have taken a variety of forms. They represent responses to very different pressures, not all of them economic. The simultaneous creation of an uniform tier of administration across a whole country, as happened in rather weak form in France, is by no means the only European model on offer.

In the Netherlands, for example, decentralisation plans have not aimed to strengthen the traditional intermediate tier of 'regional' councils, the provinces. Instead, national governments and city authorities have led attempts to develop voluntary arrangements between municipal authorities at the metropolitan or urban–regional scale as a precursor to more formal arrangements which would be at the expense of the provinces. The Dutch government is attempting to use the carrot of decentralised power and resources selectively to create governing arrangements which might enhance the economic competitiveness only of the country's most internationally connected urban centres. The big city authorities favour such moves as they promise a better deal from national government. It has also become increasingly clear to them that city–suburb rivalry exacerbates rather than solves the problems they face. Economic competitiveness is high on the institutional reform agenda in this case. But the proposed solution does not involve the creation of a new, comprehensive and uniform system of regional government.

The Dutch model, of geographically selective rather than comprehensive reform, was tried earlier and rather more successfully in Spain. This was at the regional rather than metropolitan scale but it responded primarily to cultural and political, not purely economic, pressures. The Spanish model of granting powers and resources to the autonomous communities depending on the level of demand and cultural homogeneity has sparked much interest in the UK. The 'devolution on demand' proposal for English regions considered by the Labour party, for example, reflect the same principles. It suggests that enhanced regional autonomy can be more appropriate in some regions than others and that a 'messy' system, in which regions have different status, is not necessarily a bad one. The importance of cultural, rather than purely economic, factors to regionalism is further borne out by the example of Belgium. There, a series of decentralisation proposals have developed in the attempt to balance the demands of the country's two linguistic groups against the anomalous position of Brussels (Evans, 1994).

These examples show that change in Europe is not uniform. There is a trend towards decentralisation but it is much more patchy than is often claimed. Sub-national autonomy has been strengthened, but not always at regional level. Decentralisation has not just responded to economic change. Nor is it designed explicitly to enhance regional economic competitiveness. It is not clear that reforms have enhanced regional authorities' control over major levers of economic development. As Scottish and Welsh nationalists recognise, national governments in both unitary and federal systems continue to have a great deal of influence over most major decisions taken by regional or local governments. EU member governments of all political persuasions retain control over major items of policy and expenditure. They also continue to operate relatively strong fiscal equalisation policies. Both place important limits upon sub-national autonomy.

Even in Germany, where the bulk of domestic policy decisions are dealt with by the Länder, major capital expenditures and regional development programmes have to be negotiated between the Länder and Federal government departments. Whilst the 'independent' development efforts of the Land government in Baden-Württemberg, in particular, have reached almost mythical proportions in the literature (Cooke et al, 1995), the influence wielded over Länder decisions by the Federal authorities has grown, not declined, over the last 30 years. That influence is reinforced by the equalisation system which effectively forces the transfer of huge resources from rich to poor regions. The rich western Länder, for example, could not insulate themselves from the fiscal austerity caused by the reorientation of public expenditure towards eastern Germany after reunification (Sturm, 1992). The autonomy enjoyed by the Länder compares favourably with that of other European regional administrations. But the role of national government in setting the context for regional development should not be ignored. Nor should it be assumed that all Länder are central players in regional economic development or that their strength stems wholly from their constitutional status (Sturm, 1994).

Two cheers for regional democracy

The UK evidence presented in this study supports the growing view that regional institutional capacity matters to economic performance (Cheshire, 1990; Rhodes, 1995b; Moore 1995). But there are a range of views on whether regional *government* would improve matters further. The strongest commitment to further democratisation – in Scotland and Wales – occurs where institutional structures to support economic development are already strongest. And the arguments for change there are not primarily economic; they are about the right to self-determination. By contrast, in the two English case study regions the desire for stronger economic development institutions is much more of an issue, particularly in the North East. Support for stronger economic institutions is not limited to proponents of regional government. It is very noticeable in England that supporters of regional government assume that regions would attain the mix and strength of institutions enjoyed by Scotland and Wales, and that economic performance would be enhanced, in any change.

In Scotland and Wales, by contrast, there is only minority support for the status quo which appears so attractive to English regionalists. Instead, there is popular belief that further democratisation is a good in itself and a vague expectation that it would also trigger positive economic change. Those who favour a devolved Parliament or Assembly to oversee the work of existing Scottish and Welsh government machinery expect that economic change would follow upon shifts in policy, brought about by politicians in Cardiff and Edinburgh rather than London, which would better reflect national circumstances. But for nationalists, changes of the desired order appear impossible while Westminster and Whitehall still have a hand in the distribution of resources and the determination of major policy issues. They are seen as possible only if Scottish and Welsh governments have the sole right to tax and spend in accordance with their own priorities (SNP, 1992b). It depends upon secesssion and the creation of national, not regional, governments.

The evidence from the case studies suggests there is a positive correlation between strong regional institutional capacity, regionalist cultures and sentiments and economic adjustment. The research could not, of course, fully test the stronger regionalist claim that regional *government* aids the quest for economic innovation and growth. It did suggest that the modest, additional regional autonomy enjoyed in Scotland and Wales helped in packaging resources and in the definition and delivery of regional economic strategies and programmes which had greater impacts than in the English regions. Beyond the case studies, however, there are arguments which both contradict and support the idea that regional government is important to economic competitiveness.

One basic judgement is that regional government structures cannot be decisive in improving economic fortunes since there are very marked contrasts in regional economic performance in countries with strong regional government systems. If the same system of government produces two or more economic outcomes, then something other than the system alone must explain the variation. A more sophisticated view is that variety in outcomes is evidence of autonomy. A high level of regional autonomy creates significant potential to influence economic change. Regional government may fail to utilise this potential. It may even use it in ways which impede economic innovation and growth. But the positive potential is still there. On this view, the same system would be expected to produce very different outcomes since it is premised on a high level of autonomy. Autonomy gives regions the capacity to make very different choices and pursue them, for good or ill, with powerful policy instruments. Variation in economic performance in regions whose governments choose different paths therefore underlines the influence of regional autonomy rather than denying it.

The wider European experience suggests that the latter argument is more powerful. But the extra ingredient that regional democracy adds to strong regional institutions is never defined. Commentators argue that regional government is necessary, for example, to define coherent socio-economic areas which internalise economic benefits and costs, to create legitimate constituencies of interest and reduce intergovernmental conflict, to create executive capacity to implement policy measures and to offer a one stop shop to "increase the viability of private sector involvement in the economic development process" (Cheshire, D'Arcy and Giussani, 1992: 360).

Closer examination reveals difficulties with such arguments. On the one hand, real-world systems of regional government do not have all the advantages of their theoretical cousins. On the other, it is doubtful whether some of the properties claimed for regional government are intrinsic either to democratically elected authorities or to regional levels of administration. Many arguments simply ascribe the contributions of a wide range of other agencies to the presence of regional governments. Others implicitly accept that what regional governments deliver in support of economic innovation can also be provided by government at other levels, by non-elected public agencies, by the market, by hybrid public–private organisations and by informal interorganisational networking arrangements. Even advocates of regionalism accept this is the case in arguing, for example, that "regional government assists the process of [economic] adjustment, even where such government is not regionally accountable" (Cooke, 1995).

What remains untested is whether regional governments are more effective than any other possible arrangement. The tentative advances in research on the relation between sub-national institutions and economic performance have so far been dominated by deductive approaches. They first identify sub-national economic 'hot spots' and then work backwards in an attempt to explain their success (for examples and reviews, see Amin, 1992; Amin and Thrift, 1994; Beccatini and Sengenberger, 1990; Cooke, 1995; Cooke and Morgan, 1993; de Vet, 1993; Rhodes, 1995; Sengenberger, 1993; Storper, 1993). Such accounts can be overly descriptive and difficult to compare. More empirical work, which starts from institutions and attempts to trace out their economic effects, is clearly needed. The main arguments of the deductive literature nonetheless make interesting reading.

The broad factors which are seen to encourage strong economic performance at sub-national level include:

supply-side factors: highly skilled, flexible workforces; provision of 'real services' to firms by generous (often public or non-profit) suppliers who are not themselves competitors; presence of scientifically advanced higher education sector; current or historical economic specialism(s) and clusters of activity on which to build; specialist but shared local knowledge, creating barriers to entry; dense pattern of subcontracting between key economic agents, serviced by active middlemen and brokers channelling information to buyers and sellers/producers;

technological factors: dedicated technological institutes, research and development facilities; formalised education–business links; heavy investment in scientific higher education, basic and applied research facilities, technology transfer centres; advanced programmes of technological support for small and medium-sized enterprises; basic vocational and advanced technological training for individuals;

institutional factors: presence of regional or local development agencies drawing on the support of local authorities, industry associations, trades unions and educationalists; active trades associations, chambers of commerce and craft-based organisations; providers of specialist training; regional banking structures; dense networks of associations and self-governing groups within civil society able to take on civic leadership tasks;

behavioural/cultural factors: importance of 'soft infrastructure'; traditions of interpersonal cooperation, based on agreements, custom, reputation, competitive strength; commitment to inter-firm cooperation as well as competition as a means to overcome market problems; traditions of networking between institutions and between public and private sectors; communal traditions; cultural commitment to scientific knowledge and individual advancement through learning; paternalistic large firms; employer commitment to training; close relationships between higher education and local industry; trust, resulting in the rapid communication of useful, specialist or highly contemporary knowledge; traditions of unselfish dialogue and associative behaviour through, for example, expert commissions, conferences, formal and informal consultation on government decisions;

scale factors: subsidiarity; reasonably small units of organisation and decision – the 'everyone knows everyone else' scenario which helps deepen mutual trust.

This long list confirms that many factors other than those directly attributable to regional government affect regional economic performance. Of course, it is possible to invoke 'chicken and egg' arguments: that the creation of regional government provides a platform on which other things, such as regional banking structures, can develop. But all such arguments can be reversed; why create regional government, for example, if what one wants is regional banks? The importance of a wide range of non-institutional factors, reflecting highly specific economic histories, makes some commentators pessimistic about the transfer of innovative economic milieu from one place to another:

> [M]any of the conditions for success....are not readily transferable...Key success factors – such as a pioneering role in innovation in new or niche markets, a well developed and integrated institutional support framework for entrepreneurship and social traditions encouraging the accumulation and exchange of know-how, skill and information.....are not easily created by the traditional instruments of spatial policy....[A] new model of growth cannot be simply 'plucked out' of its spatial context and implanted in areas which lack the institutional and social environment for such growth.
> (Amin, 1992:132)

Such arguments deserve to be taken seriously. It would be a little hopeful, for example, to expect that the decentralisation of higher education funding and policy to regional level in the UK, simply because it mirrored the institutional pattern in Germany, would immediately elevate the performance and industrial relevance of UK universities in science and technology to German levels. More decentralised decision making in higher education funding can result in more university support for regional industry. Indeed the experience of the recently created Higher Education Funding Councils for Scotland and Wales arguably lends support for this argument. But on one hand, this can clearly happen without regionally elected authorities. On the other, the powerful German commitment to advanced technical education and to links between higher education and businesses is not something that will be developed overnight in the UK, no matter who is in control of higher education policy. What all such examples suggest is the need for an understanding of regional economic innovation to precede and inform institutional change. This would demand a more sophisticated analysis of the factors driving economic change and, in all probability, a more limited and sharply defined approach towards institutional design.

Institutions, networks and regional development

Much of the impetus for structural change in the UK is not built on clear evidence that more regional autonomy produces better government or greater prosperity. More likely, it illustrates dissatisfaction with the way recent UK governments have treated the poorer regions and the non-English nations, politically as well as economically. It signals resentment at the way local government responsibilities have been usurped by quangos. And it suggests growing regional perceptions that moves toward different models of governance might benefit regions, partly because of feelings that access to EU resources would be easier. These reactive impulses do not provide a solid basis on which to build substantial structural change. They leave open other, less drastic, institutional possibilities. Many of the substantive demands of regionalists might be achieved, for example, if certain English regions possessed the successful economic development institutions that Scotland and Wales have, if they were supported and orchestrated by a central administration more committed to recognising distinctive regional needs and potentials, and if they were bolstered by reinvigorated local governments.

But institutional frameworks in any case only partially explain different patterns of economic dynamism. The argument that the road to economic success lies in having the 'right' institutional structures and modes of representation is increasingly challenged by another which argues that a locality's – and not necessarily a region's – 'soft infrastructure' matters most. This alternative approach focuses more upon the way ideas, people and ways of working are thrown up by particular local environments and cultures than upon representative structures. In the terms used here, there is as much concern with *autonomy to* as there is with *autonomy from*. Regional – or local – government autonomy from higher levels of authority can clearly help create the capacity for independent action. But there is no guarantee that sub-national political control will necessarily lead to better economic outcomes. What matters is the capacity to agree upon and achieve general economic goals.

This process is not simply about formal structures of representation or the placing of functions at the 'right' spatial level. It is about finding an appropriate balance between politics and markets. It involves fusing the capacity of all relevant partners – at different levels of government and within the public and private sectors – to act in a common cause, or at least to support particular actions within a broadly shared approach. Without this, formal autonomy means very little. With it, limitations to institutional autonomy can be overcome. This more fluid conception of autonomy is difficult to pin down. But contemporary research and the debate about the merits of regional institutional change can benefit from taking it more seriously. It demands different ways of understanding and acting, for example in the use of negotiating skills rather than authority. It focuses attention on a capacity for economic innovation that is built upon consensual ideas and the commitment of a wide range of interest groups, not just on formal structures of decision making.

This report does not argue against regional government in England or devolution/independence for Scotland and Wales per se. Where there has been sustained hostility toward the status quo by the peoples of a region or nation, irrespective of the political hue of the government of the day, then there are clearly strong *democratic* arguments for change. Democracies, after all, are meant to respond to the wishes of electorates, whether or not the result is better economic performance. The argument of this research project is that the link between elected regional government and increased economic innovation and growth remains unproven and underexplored. As a result, any argument for regional government which relies solely upon an economic justification currently lacks strength. Whilst we may not like it, the links between economic success and formal democracy seem, for the moment, to be loosening rather than tightening.

Even if one ignores the fact that 'regional' means very different things in different countries, the link between democratic decision making at the regional level and economic competitiveness is very uncertain. If one of the goals of institutional change in Britain is to establish the conditions for stronger economic performance, the creation of regional government in England or the granting of further devolution or even independence to Scotland and Wales represents a leap of faith. This leap might be justifiable in democratic terms but there seem to be a number of alternative, less disruptive and potentially less costly options available.

As one of the people asked by the project to analyse the relationship between sub-national institutions and economic development argued, "the British disease is forever proposing institutional solutions to organic problems". It is a disease whose effects can be seen, particularly, in the bewildering number of recent changes to sub-national governmental structures and to economic development institutions in recent years. It is at least arguable, then, that what is required at the present time is not a headlong rush into further institutional change but a deeper discussion about the organic options for change.

A number of positive things might emerge from a more organic approach to key issues in regional economic development. First, the nature and boundaries of the problem might be better explored and defined. An open debate about issues is always likely to be more productive than a sensitive one about structures which too often results in all the interested parties simply defending their turf. Second, organic solutions, based on networking and the forming of relations between institutions rather than their abolition or reform, can 'bind in' a wider constituency and hence deepen the level of support for regional actions. Third, even if organic options are ultimately adjudged inappropriate, a more limited set of institutional changes, specifically related to the promotion of particular aspects of regional economic innovation and development, might emerge. The evidence from the case studies covered in this report is that the organic debate is beginning to happen, in UK regions and nations and elsewhere. It would be a pity if it were drowned out by louder and cruder voices clamouring for constitutional and institutional reforms which might promise more than they can deliver.

References

Aitken, K. (1992) 'The economy', in Linklater, M. and Denniston, R. (eds), *Anatomy of Scotland: how Scotland works*, Edinburgh: Chambers: 230-333.

Amin, A. (1992) 'Big firms versus the regions', in Dunford, M. and Kafkalas, G. (eds), *Cities and regions in the new Europe*, London: Belhaven.

Amin, A. (ed) (1994) *Post-Fordism: a reader*, Oxford: Blackwell.

Amin, A. and Malmberg, A. (1992) 'Competing structural and institutional influences on the geography of production in Europe', *Environment and Planning A*, vol 24: 401-16.

Amin, A. and Thrift, N. (eds) (1994) *Globalization, institutions and regional development in Europe*, Oxford: OUP.

Anderson, J.A. (1990) 'Skeptical reflections on a Europe of Regions: Britain, Germany and the ERDF', *Journal of Public Policy*, vol 10, no 4: 417-47.

Beccatini, G. and Sengenberger, W. (1990) *Industrial districts*, Geneva: ILO.

Bennett, R.J. (ed) (1990) *Decentralisation, local government and markets: towards a post-welfare agenda?*, Oxford: OUP.

Burch, M. (1993) 'The political dimension: the scope for a regional initiative?', in Burch and Rhodes (eds), 'The North West region and Europe': 46-54.

Burch, M. and Holliday, I. (1993) 'Institutional emergence: the case of the North West region of England', *Regional Policy and Politics*, vol 3, no 2: 29-50.

Burch, M. and Rhodes, M. (eds) (1993) 'The North West region and Europe: development of a regional strategy', EPRU Paper 3/93, Manchester: European Policy Research Unit, University of Manchester.

CBI Scotland (1995) Scottish business agenda for a more prosperous Scotland, Glasgow: CBI Scotland.

CBI Scottish Manufacturing Group (1994) *Manufacturing matters*, Glasgow: CBI.

Cheshire, P.E. (1990) 'Explaining the recent performance of the European Community's major urban regions', *Urban Studies*, vol 27: 311-33.

Cheshire, P.E., D'Arcy, E. and Giussani, B. (1992) 'Purpose built for failure? Local, regional and national government in Britain', *Environment and Planning C: Government and Policy*, vol 10: 355-69.

Cooke, P. (ed) (1995) *The rise of the rustbelt*, London: UCL Press.

Cooke, P. (1994) 'The co-operative advantage of regions', paper presented to the conference on 'Regions, Institutions And Technology: Reorganizing Economic Geography in Canada and the Anglo-American World', University of Toronto, September.

Cooke, P. and Morgan, K. (1993) 'The network paradigm: new departures in corporate and regional development', *Environment and Planning D: Society and Space*, vol 11: 543-64.

Cooke, P., Price, A. and Morgan, K. (1995) 'Regulating regional economies: Wales and Baden-Württemberg in transition', in Rhodes (ed), *The regions and the new Europe*: 105-35.

Coulson, A. (1990) 'Devolving power: the case for regional government', *Fabian Tract 537*, London: Fabian Society.

Commission for Local Democracy (1995) *Taking charge: the rebirth of local democracy*, London: Municipal Journal Books.

Crouch, C. and Marquand, D. (eds) (1989) *The new centralism: Britain out of step in Europe?*, Oxford: Blackwell.

Davis, H. and Stewart, J. (1993) *The growth of government by appointment: implications for local democracy*, Luton: Local Government Management Board.

de Vet, J. (1993) 'Globalization and local and regional competitiveness', *STI Review*, vol 13: 89-121.

Dicken, P., Forsgren, M. and Malmberg, A. (1994) 'The local embeddedness of transnational corporations', in Amin and Thrift (eds), *Globalization, institutions and regional development in Europe*: 24-45.

European Dialogue/Friedrich Ebert Foundation (1993) 'Power to the people? Economic self-determination and the regions', Proceedings of a conference on 'Regional Economic Policy and Regional Government in the UK', European Dialogue/Friedrich Ebert Foundation.

Evans, R. (1994) 'Brussels', in Harding, A., Dawson, J., Evans, R. and Parkinson, M. (eds), *European cities in the 1990s: profiles, policies and prospects*, Manchester: Manchester University Press.

Fairley, J. (1990) 'The impact of the Scottish Enterprise reforms on vocational education and training', *Regional Studies*, vol 24, no 4: 363-66.

Fairley, J. (1992) 'Scottish local authorities and Local Enterprise Companies;: a developing relationship?', *Regional Studies*, vol 26, no 2: 193-99.

Garside, P.L. and Hebbert, M. (eds) (1989) *British regionalism 1900-2000*, London: Mansell.

Harding, A. and Le Galès, P. (1996) 'Globalization, urban change and urban policy', in Scott, A. (ed), *The limits of globalization*, London: Routledge.

Harvie, C. (1994) *The rise of regional Europe*, London: Routledge.

Hayton, K. (1992) 'Scottish Enterprise: a challenge to local land-use planning?', *Town Planning Review*, vol 63, no 3: 265-78.

Hill, S. and Munday, M. (1991) 'The determinants of inward investment: a Welsh analysis', *Applied Economics*, vol 23, no 11: 1761-70.

HMSO (1993) *Scotland in the Union: a partnership for good*, Cm 2225, Edinburgh: HMSO.

Hogwood, B. (1995) 'The integrated regional offices and the Single Regeneration Budget', Commission for Local Democracy, Report no 13, London: CLD.

Jessop, B. (1994) *Post-Fordism and the state*, in Amin (ed), *Post-Fordism and the state*.

Jones, B. and Keating, M. (eds) (1995) *The European Union and the Regions*, Oxford: Clarendon.

Jones, G. (1988) Against regional government, *Local Government Studies* (Sept/Oct): 1-11.

Keating, M. (1992) 'Regional autonomy in the changing state order: a framework for analysis', *Regional Politics and Policy*, vol 2, no 3: 45-61.

Labour Party (1995) *A choice for England: a consultation paper on Labour's plans for English regional government*, London: Labour Party.

Le Galès, P. (1994) 'Regions' economic policy: an alternative to French Jacobinism?', *Regional Policy and Politics*, vol 3, no 4.

Lee, C.H. (1995) *Scotland and the United Kingdom: the economy and the union in the twentieth* century, Manchester: Manchester University Press.

Luard, E. (1990) *The globalization of politics*, London: Macmillan.

Mayer, M. (1994) 'Post-Fordism in city politics', in Amin (ed), *Post-Fordism and the state*.

McCalman, J. (1992) 'Setting up in Silicon Glen: inward investment and implications for spin-off and supplier linkages', *Environment and Planning C: Government and Policy*, vol 10: 423-38.

McCrone, D. (1992) *Understanding Scotland: the sociology of a stateless nation*, London: Routledge.

McCrone, D. (1993) 'Regionalism and constitutional change in Scotland', *Regional Studies*, vol 27, no 6: 507-12.

Midwinter, A., Keating, M. and Mitchell, J. (1991) *Politics and public policy in Scotland*, London: Macmillan.

Mitchell, J. (1995) 'Lobbying 'Brussels': the case of Scotland Europa', *European Urban and Regional Studies*, vol 2, no 4: 1-12.

Moore, C. (1995) 'Scotland and the SDA', in Rhodes (ed), *The regions and the new Europe*: 229-46.

Moore, C. and Booth, S. (1989) Managing competition: meso-corporatism, pluralism and the negotiated order in Scotland, Oxford: Clarendon.

Morgan, K. and Roberts, E. (1993) 'The democratic deficit: a guide to quangoland', Papers in Planning Research 144, Department of City and Regional Planning, University of Wales in Cardiff.

Murphy, P. and Caborn, R. (1995) Regional government for England – an economic imperative, Sheffield, PAVIC, Sheffield Hallam University.

Ohmae, K. (1993) 'The rise of the region state', *Foreign Affairs*: 78-87.

Parry, R. (1993) 'Towards a democratised Scottish Office?', *Scottish Affairs*, no 5: 41-57.

Paterson, L. (1994) *The autonomy of modern Scotland*, Edinburgh: Edinburgh University Press.

Peck, J. (1993) 'The North West economy: catching up or falling behind?', in Burch and Rhodes (eds), 'The North West region and Europe':32-45.

Pieda (1993) *Regional economic strategy for North West England: final report*, Manchester: Pieda.

Rhodes, M. (ed) (1995) *The regions and the new Europe: patterns in core and periphery development*, Manchester: Manchester University Press.

Rhodes, M. (1995a) 'Introduction: the regions and the new Europe', in Rhodes (ed), *The regions and the new Europe*: 1-26.

Rhodes, M. (1995b) 'Conclusion: the viability of regional strategies', in Rhodes (ed), *The regions and the new Europe*: 329-51.

Rhodes, R.A.W. (1988) *Beyond Westminster and Whitehall: the sub-central governments of Britain*, London: Unwin Hyman.

Salt, H. (1994) 'Taking control of regional government', *Municipal Review and AMA News*, no 753: 198-99.

Scottish Affairs Committee (1995) *The operation of the Enterprise Agencies and the LECs*, Cmnd 339 I-III (3 vols), London: HMSO.

Scottish Council, Development and Industry (SCDI) (1993) *Development strategy: a consultative paper for members*, Edinburgh: SCDI.

Scottish National Party (SNP) (1992a) *Independence in Europe: make it happen now!*, Edinburgh: SNP.

Scottish National Party (1992b) *Recovery in Scotland: make it happen now!*, Edinburgh: SNP.

Scottish Office (1994) *The economy of Scotland*, Factsheet 13, Edinburgh: HMSO.

Scottish Trades Union Council (STUC) (1992) *Power for change: an agenda for a Scottish Parliament*, Glasgow: STUC.

Sengenberger, W. (1993) 'Local development and international economic competition', *International Labour Review*, vol 132, no 3: 313-29.

Sharpe, L.J. (ed) (1993) *The rise of meso government in Europe*, London: Sage.

Shaw, K. (1994) 'The development of a new urban corporatism: the politics of urban regeneration in the North East of England', *Regional Studies*, vol 27, no 3: 251-59.

Stewart, J., Greer, A. and Hoggett, P. (1995) *The quango state: an alternative approach*, Commission for Local Democracy Report 10, London: CLD.

Storper, M. (1993) 'Regional "worlds" of production: learning and innovation in the technology districts of France, Italy and the USA', *Regional Studies*, vol 27, no 5: 433-55.

Sturm, R. (1992) 'The changing territiorial balance', in Smith, G., Paterson, W.E., Merki, P.H. and Padgett, S. (eds), *Developments in German politics*, London: Macmillan: 119-36.

Sturm, R. (1994) 'The political economy of German regionalism: modernisation strategies of the Länder', paper presented to the workshop on 'The Political Economy of Regionalism', European Consortium for Political Research, Madrid, April.

Tindale, S. (1995) *Devolution on demand: options for the English regions and London*, IPPR Monograph, London: Institute for Public Policy Research.

Toonen, T.A.J. (1993) 'Dutch provinces and the struggle for the meso', in Sharpe (ed), *The rise of meso government in Europe.*

Turok, I. (1993) 'Inward investment and local linkages: how deeply embedded is "Silicon Glen"?', Regional Studies, vol 27, no 5: 401-17.

Turok, I. and Richardson, R. (1991) 'External takeovers of Scottish companies in the 1980s', *Area*, vol 23, no 1.

Young, S., Hood, N. and Peters, E. (1994) 'Multinational enterprises and regional economic development', *Regional Studies*, vol 28, no 7: 657-77.

Appendix A: Changes in regional activity, 1985-95

REGIONAL ECONOMIC DEVELOPMENT AND PLANNING

Regional activity	Function	Rationale	Boundary criteria	Degree of autonomy	Distribution of power (I)
Government Regional Offices (1993) - comprised of combined regional offices of DoE, DE, DTI, DT.	Implement DoE, DE, DTI, DT national objectives; develop local partnerships and networks; administer Single Regeneration Budget (SRB).	Improve coherence of government actions; provide single point of contact for customers; use local knowledge to advise on SRB allocation; reduce overheads	Standard English regions, except for separate Office for Merseyside (10 regions).	Limited. Senior Regional Directors more power to develop appropriate local structures and processes but central sanction still vital.	= slight deconc. - role of SRB offset by resource cuts. Increased difficulty in reconciling central and regionalist demands likely.
English Partnerships regional offices (1993)	Work in consort with other regeneration agencies; work to regional strategies and liaise closely with GORs; deliver physical aspects of regeneration schemes; administer Investment Fund consolidated from previous grant regimes and top-sliced SRB monies.	Partnership ethos requires local knowledge and presence; similarly, property marketing and management; ease of contact with GORs.	Administrative convenience; amalgamation of historic regions to reduce overheads (6 regions).	Moderate. Scope for regional policy making with project appraisal, but major projects approved by main office and must meet national targets. Chief Executive keen on devolving responsibility.	= Slight devolution. Possibility of increased competition with regional inward investment agencies.

= straight increase in regional capacity
+ regionalisation (powers passed up)
- regionalisation (powers passed down)

REGIONAL ECONOMIC DEVELOPMENT AND PLANNING (contd)

Regional activity	Function	Rationale	Boundary criteria	Degree of autonomy	Distribution of power (I)
English Regional Associations (ERAs) and **Regional Planning Conferences (RPCs)** (national coverage - 1992)	Local Authority representative bodies. RPCs coordinate member authorities input to government regional planning guidance (framework for Structure Plans, related lobbying). ERAs provide a fora, lobby on broader planning, transportation, economic development and waste management issues.	Means of strategic co-operation between LAs and defend collective interests; ensure government guidance for Structure Plans reflects regional concerns and trends; in some cases strategic role in use of European programmes.	Standard English Regions (9 regions).	Usually limited. Government not obliged to follow recommendations; constrained too by degree of consensus between members and level of modest financial support, varying extent of membership. Variation in internal capacity - SE and NE - strong, E. Midlands weak.	= Modest rehabilitation of regional planning. Voluntaristic nature of bodies. Lack of executive power at regional level to implement strategic schemes.

= straight increase in regional capacity
+ regionalisation (powers passed up)
- regionalisation (powers passed down)

PRIVATISED UTILITIES AND THEIR REGULATORS

Regional activity	Function	Rationale	Boundary criteria	Degree of autonomy	Distribution of power (I)
Water companies and OFWAT (1989/90); regional electricity companies and OFFER, (1990/91).	Provision of utilities, investment in infrastructure subject to regulators' price controls given certain costs, revenues and service standards.	Separation of intra-regional from national supply arrangements to avoid regional suppliers gaining monopoly advantages and regulation to protect customers' interests.	Mixture of administrative, hydrological and historic factors. Boundaries of regulators' regional offices not always synonymous with utility companies.	Considerable increase case of regional utilities - only controlled through price mechanism. Shift from service distribution, customer services, marketing to executive decision making. Regional offices of regulators limited - informational and advisory role only.	+ water - electricity Loss of local political control of water but increase in executive power in regional electricity companies, could grow further in future if multi-functional regional utility companies with vested interest in economic prospects of region.

= straight increase in regional capacity
+ regionalisation (powers passed up)
- regionalisation (powers passed down)

HOUSING

Regional activity	Function	Rationale	Boundary criteria	Degree of autonomy	Distribution of power (I)
Regional Offices of Housing Corporation (1964) - 2 new Regional Offices in SE (1995)	Develop regional strategy for Housing Association activity, approve projects, allocate funds and monitor performance. Each regions capital programme included in national Approved Development Programme (ADP).	Creation of two new regions and adjustment of boundaries to match those of GORs.	GOR boundaries (now 11 regions).	Although scale of resources set by national Housing Needs Index, some scope to vary policy and funding allocations given local context and priorities. But national tightening of registration rules, reduced grant aid and tough performance criteria has recently limited autonomy.	= Greater coherence in regional decision making following introduction of joint planning arrangements to ensure RO's component of ADP dovetails with LA Housing Investment Programmes. Also regional consultative meetings set up to improve local feedback.

= straight increase in regional capacity
+ regionalisation (powers passed up)
- regionalisation (powers passed down)

FIRE

Regional activity	Function	Rationale	Boundary criteria	Degree of autonomy	Distribution of power
Fire and Civil Defence Authorities (1986)	Responsibility for provision of fire services and related civil defence, emergency planning functions. Run by Joint Boards of district nominees.	Retention of metropolitan-wide service because of efficiency and operational advantages (eg economies of scale - training and equipment). Possibility of close liaison with related local authority functions (eg police, building control).	Former metropolitan county boundaries.	Considerable executive powers, but Secretary of State has considerable influence - sets operational targets and can specify manpower levels (85% costs).	= Substantial continuity. Shift from direct to indirect political control has not led to accountability issues because of uncontroversial, apolitical nature of service . (1)

= straight increase in regional capacity
+ regionalisation (powers passed up)
- regionalisation (powers passed down)

POLICE

Regional activity	Function	Rationale	Boundary criteria	Degree of autonomy	Distribution of power (I)
Joint Police Authorities (1986)	Ensuring adequate and efficient law enforcement by determining budget, staffing levels and senior appointments. Run by district nominees (1/2) appointees (1/3) and magistrates (1/6) - Recently Home Secretary has introduced appointees.	Ensuring accountability and sensitivity to local concerns. Tripartite system of control aims to maintain balance between efficiency and democratic accountability. Recently, increased intervention by Secretary of State.	Former metropolitan county (except London) boundaries. (5 regions).	Considerable, but checked by Secretary of State's efficiency controls and sanctioning of expenditure and Chief Constable's executive powers of direction and legal status of employees.	= Continuity. Inter-force arrangements have successfully handled regional issues such as purchase of expensive equipment, drugs and traffic monitoring. Slight shift to centre recently with change in composition of police authorities.

= straight increase in regional capacity
+ regionalisation (powers passed up)
- regionalisation (powers passed down)

HEALTH

Regional activity	Function	Rationale	Boundary criteria	Degree of autonomy	Distribution of power (1)
Regional Health Authorities (1994)	Take overview of regional health needs; setting regional targets to ensure purchasers of health care deliver appropriate improvements and meet national objectives; research and development and training role. Managed by Boards of government appointees.	'Market management' role - handling strategic issues such as overall performance, future investment priorities, balancing purchaser, provider and professional perspectives, education and training and regional environmental hazards, briefing centre on regional picture.	Amalgamation of 14 old RHA boundaries (8 regions).	Control capital monies and may withold revenue monies if contrators fail to meet targets. Must rely on persuasion of local purchasers because of their operational powers. Also obliged to observe national targets, cost controls, pay.	= Continued bureaucratic control at intermediate regional level. Concern about lack of direct political accountability, patient input, and possibility of further centralisation if RHAs become regional offices of NHS Management Executive.
Social Services Inspectorate (1992)	Dual role: inspect social services provision to ensure it is efficient and effective and protect users' well being; policy development, monitoring implementation of legislation, central guidance.	Ensure: compliance with Citizen's Charter, by improving complaints procedures, increasing number of inspections and involving users more; rapid implementation of community care legislation by LAs.	Operational. Policy group work is split into 4 areas while Inspection group workload is divided between 6 regions.	Limited - duties and responsibilities determined by central government.	=

= straight increase in regional capacity
+ regionalisation (powers passed up)
- regionalisation (powers passed down)

EDUCATION

Regional activity	Function	Rationale	Boundary criteria	Degree of autonomy	Distribution of power (1)
Further Educational Funding Council - regional offices (1992)	National function to allocate grants to Further Education and sixth form colleges, increase proportion staying-on. Regional offices' role to ensure local provision meets needs, track proposed developments in FE establishments. Run by Boards of goverment appointees.	Regional structure necessary to ensure FE provision meets local labour market needs, preserve diversity of local provision, and provide point of contact for colleges. Adoption of same boundaries as GORs may encourage closer links between TEC/LA economic development plans and FE provision.	Standard planning regions (9 regions).	Limited. Regional committees are essentially advisory bodies and information providers. Critical decisions about funding made by Secretary of State and main council.	+ Removal of FE, tertiary and sixth form colleges from LEA control and replacement of their support services demanded that the FEFC be structured along regional lines.
Office for Standards in Education - regional offices (1992)	Improve standards of achievement and quality of education by monitoring teaching standards and performance of schools and regulating the work of independent registered inspectors.	Regional structure preferable for agreeing programmes of inspection with schools, provision of information to parents and following up issues raised.	Enable regulatory tasks to be performed more easily (14 areas).	Limited. Regional offices are essentially administrative arms of a department with national goals and standards which mainly perform a monitoring and feedback role.	=

| Funding Agency for Schools - regional structure (1994) | Distributes and monitors grants to grant maintained schools and planning and providing secondary school places, in most instances in conjunction with LAs. Run by Board of Government appointees. | Plan provision and encouraging switch to grant maintained status. Regional organisation of monitoring and planning ensures personal contact, builds local knowledge, discover parents' needs and facilitate devolved management. | Operational, may grow in number if more schools opt out (6 regions). | Considerable power and discretion, subject to level of resources from DfE. | + Powers shifted from LEA to quango. Its regional structure mimics LEA's local knowledge and technical expertise in the hope the latter will be completely supplanted. |

= straight increase in regional capacity
+ regionalisation (powers passed up)
- regionalisation (powers passed down)

NEXT STEPS AGENCIES

Regional activity	Function	Rationale	Boundary criteria	Degree of autonomy	Distribution of power (1)
- With provincial offices (eg Employment Service, Highways Agency, Inland Revenue, Child Support Agency, Valuation Office - total of 17). Established progressively since 1988.	Various. Carry out executive functions of Civil Service in line with contractual guidelines and performance targets and Citizen's Charter.	Improving efficiency and effectiveness of Civil Service by restructuring: separating policy making from executive functions, delegating more management responsibility, ensure citizen contact.	Various. Usually defined on operational basis - administrative convenience or number of customers - or for historical reasons.	Little discretion on policy matters but considerable scope in method of implementation. Growing concern about lack of parliamentary accountability of NSAs.	- Slight decentralisation of executive responsibility but not financial control and policy making functions.

= straight increase in regional capacity
+ regionalisation (powers passed up)
- regionalisation (powers passed down)

THE ARTS

Regional activity	Function	Rationale	Boundary criteria	Degree of autonomy	Distribution of power (I)
Regional Arts Boards (1991)	Implement national objectives of Arts Council of England (raise profile of different art forms, increase public accessibility, liaise with main funding agencies, partners), offer grant aid, handle educational and outreach work.	Greater responsibility for allocating funds in order to respond to local distinctiveness and talent, avoid central bureaucracy and involvement in detail, relate spending to LA and others' plans.	Based on old Regional Arts Association boundaries except for two mergers. Broadly similar to standard planning regions but major differences in SE and E. Midlands (10).	Discretion over finding growing, greater regional networking but tighter expenditure controls and guidance from ACE who have shown reluctance to devolve funding. 90% of funds from ACE.	- Modest decentralisation but mismatch between responsibilities and powers. Growing issue about regional distribution of Lottery monies (c £120m-1995/96).

= straight increase in regional capacity
+ regionalisation (powers passed up)
- regionalisation (powers passed down)

TOURISM

Regional activity	Function	Rationale	Boundary criteria	Degree of autonomy	Distribution of power (I)
Regional Tourist Boards (1969)	Promotion regional tourist industry, financial support, customer care, marketing, research. Ensure integration regional and national strategies.	Delegation of greater financial responsibility intended to promote local networking and partnership. Underlying logic one of making diminished resources go further.	Loosely based upon standard regions but SE split into 4 and North into Cumbria and Northumbria (11 regions).	Diminishing, modest resource base but growing discretion - recently given greater delegated powers to co-fund partnership ventures.	- Modest deconcentration of executive responsibility.

= straight increase in regional capacity
+ regionalisation (powers passed up)
- regionalisation (powers passed down)

SPORT

Regional activity	Function	Rationale	Boundary criteria	Degree of autonomy	Distribution of power (I)
Regional Councils of Sport and Recreation (1960s)	Further national objectives (promotion knowledge, practice, high standards, support/ provide facilities) prepare regional strategies, allocate grants.	Contact with local partners, strategic guidance to local authorities on sport and recreation plans.	Based on aggregations of English counties.	Discretion over grant awards within centrally defined expenditure ceilings.	= But regional strategies likely to become more important because of scale of resources from National Lottery to Sports Council (£125m 1995/96).

= straight increase in regional capacity
+ regionalisation (powers passed up)
- regionalisation (powers passed down)

Appendix B

List of individuals whose views were drawn upon for the study

All affiliations are accurate as at summer 1995 (the interview period).

K. Aitken, Freelance journalist and former Industrial Editor, The Scotsman

J. Armstrong, Industrial Advisor to the Government Office for the North East and Northern Development Company

G. Baird, Executive Director, Scottish Financial Enterprise and former Chief Executive, Scotland Europa

H. Bernstein, Deputy Chief Executive, Manchester City Council

P. Bounds, Chief Executive, Liverpool City Council

R. Craig Campbell, Chief Economist, Scottish Council (Development and Industry)

Sir A. Cockshaw, Chairman, AMEC plc and joint chairman, North West Business Leadership Team

Prof P. Cooke, School for Advanced Studies in the Social Sciences, University of Wales in Cardiff

H. Conway, Chief Executive, Cardiff Chamber of Commerce and Industry

K. Davies, Chief Executive, Plaid Cymru

P. Denham Regional Director, Government Office for the North East

A.N.A. Dicken, Teesside Site Manager, ICI

L. Ellmann, Leader, Lancashire County Council

J. Elvidge, Under-Secretary, Scottish Office Industry Department

Dr A. Foord, Director, North East CBI

T. Gernon, Head of Corporate Affairs, Teeside Training and Enterprise Council

C. Gibaud, Chief Executive, Mersey Partnership

L. Gold, Chief Executive, Scottish CBI

J. Graham, Under-Secretary, Scottish Office Environment Department

P. Price, Head of European Affairs Division, WDA

G. Price-Jones, Secretary, Council of Welsh Districts

Prof B. Robson, Geography Department, University of Manchester

G. Robson, Under-Secretary, Scottish Office Industry Department

A senior spokesperson, Industry Department, Welsh Office

P. Shakeshaft, Director of Corporate Affairs, Northern Development Company

Sir J. C. Shaw, Deputy Governor, Bank of Scotland

P. Sheldon (with F. Cuthbert), Chief Executive, South Glamorgan TEC

M. Shukman, Head of Co-ordinating Division, WDA

J. Snaith, Economic Development Officer, Chief Executives' Department, Sunderland City Council

J. Tomaney, A. Pyke and D. Charles, Centre for Urban and Regional Development Studies, University of Newcastle

T. Thomas, Chief Executive, The Co-operative Bank

I. Turok, Centre for Planning, Strathclyde University

D. Walsh, Chair, Economic Development Committee, Cleveland County Council

Prof J. Ward, IBM UK

E. Weeple, Under-Secretary, Scottish Office Industry Department

T. Wetherby, Chairman, INWARD

J. Wright, Economic Development Officer, Development Department, Newcastle City Council

J. Hamilton, Economic Development Officer, Northumberland County Council

J. Hansen, EC Commissioner for Wales

D. Henshaw, Chief Executive, Knowsley Borough Council

M. Hollingsworth, Chief Planner, Land Authority for Wales

J. Harris and J. Jones, Convention of Scottish Local Authorities

Prof N. Hood, Marketing Deptartment, Strathclyde University (formerly of Locate in Scotland)

R. Howarth, Director, Wales Quality Centre

Prof. J. Hughes, Development Director, Development Board for Rural Wales

E. Haywood, Director, CBI Wales

R. Howard, Regional Secretary, TUC Northern Region

D. Jenkins, Director, Wales TUC

N. Jones, Assistant Secretary, Assembly of Welsh Counties

S. Knighton, Director, Business in the Community, Wales

R. Leonard, Assistant Secretary, Scottish TUC

J. Lewis, Lecturer, Geography Department, University of Durham

G. Lord, Kellogg UK Ltd.

J. Lord, Director of Strategy, Scottish Enterprise

J. Madden, Chief Executive, The Engineering Centre for Wales

D. McCrone, Sociology Department, University of Edinburgh

A. McKenzie, Chief Planner, Scottish Office Environment Department

N. Meachen, Deputy Secretary, North of England Assembly of Local Authorities

P. Mitchell, Welsh Development Agency

J. Moorhouse, Director, Scottish Business in the Community

B. Morgan (with J. Atkinson), Chief Economist, Welsh Development Agency

Prof K. Morgan, Department of City and Regional Planning, University of Wales in Cardiff

P. Nicholls, Manager, World Trade Centre

G. Parker, Senior Business Advisor, Tyne and Wear Development Corporation

G. Piper, Chief Executive, North West Business Leadership Team

K. Richardson, North East Chamber of Commerce